The Classic
era of
American
Pulp Magazines

FOR
PHILIPPA & PAM
WITH LOVE

The Classic
era of
American
Pulp Magazines

Peter Haining

CHICAGO
REVIEW
PRESS

Library of Congress Cataloging-in-Publication Data
Is available from the Library of Congress.

Cover design: Jon Gray
Pulp image work: Chris Scott

First U.S. edition published in 2001 by Chicago Review Press, Incorporated
814 North Franklin Street
Chicago, Illinois 60610
1-55652-389-0

Printed in Singapore

5 4 3 2 1

First published in Great Britain by Prion Books Limited

Contents

SEPTEMBER

Weird Tales

Satan's Palimpsest

an eery tale of sinister doom

By SEABURY QUINN

CLARK ASHTON SMITH
EDMOND HAMILTON
H. P. LOVECRAFT

The
No. 1 Magazine
of
STRANGE
and
UNUSUAL
Stories

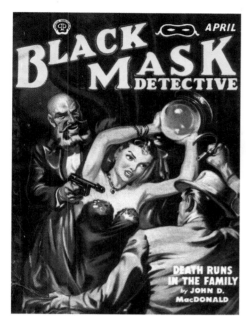

OPPOSITE

*The garishly
imaginative art of
Margaret Brundage
is forever associated
with* Weird Tales.
*(September, 1937)
(See page 106)*

ABOVE

*Rudolph Belarski
was among*
Black Mask's
*most evocative
cover artists.
(April, 1939)
(See page 58)*

Foreword

I saw my first pulp magazines heaped up on a counter in the U.K. chain store Woolworths in the early 1950s. The brilliant red and yellow covers, with their illustrations of violent action and beautiful girls in various stages of disarray, immediately caught my fervent schoolboy imagination. So, instead of spending my weekly pocket money on sweets and the usual comic, I purchased a copy of a magazine called *Weird Tales*. I walked home, my head lost in worlds of fantasy and horror, and somehow knew I would never be quite the same again.

It would, in fact, be a while before I came to appreciate the uniqueness of these American magazines, shipped across the Atlantic and sold cut price in various outlets such as Woolworths – and a lot longer before I learned about their history. I did soon discover, though, that they were not approved reading by my parents, and any copies of *Weird Tales* – and another favorite, *Black Mask* – that I could afford had to be secreted away for reading by flashlight under the bedclothes. Little did I realize then that there had been teenagers just like me doing exactly the same thing in the United States, a generation earlier.

In the 50 years since then, I have constantly been on the lookout for copies of these remarkable magazines – becoming ever rarer by the year – and now own a quite substantial archive, which has helped to make this book possible. Sadly, my first copy of *Weird Tales* has long since disappeared – left behind in the loft of one of the family houses when we moved, I believe – but the memory of the magazine, the words, and the pictures, linger on. It was a purchase of the purest chance that opened the doors into the unique world of the pulps. A golden era, I believe you will agree, after journeying through the pages that follow.

PETER HAINING, LONDON, APRIL 2000

THRILLS
INCORPORATED

MURDER in TOMORROW
by ROGER GARRADINE

MEETING on MARS
by DURHAM KEYS

No 6
1/-

Big Shots *and* Cheap Thrills

INTRODUCTION

The pulp magazines were all about three things: action, adventure, and sex – not necessarily together or in that order.

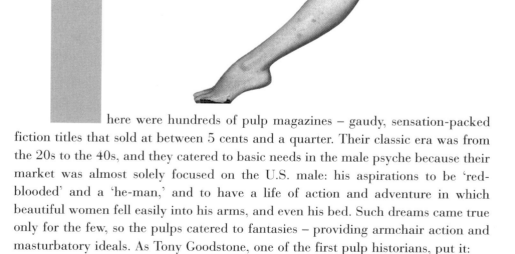

There were hundreds of pulp magazines – gaudy, sensation-packed fiction titles that sold at between 5 cents and a quarter. Their classic era was from the 20s to the 40s, and they catered to basic needs in the male psyche because their market was almost solely focused on the U.S. male: his aspirations to be 'red-blooded' and a 'he-man,' and to have a life of action and adventure in which beautiful women fell easily into his arms, and even his bed. Such dreams came true only for the few, so the pulps catered to fantasies – providing armchair action and masturbatory ideals. As Tony Goodstone, one of the first pulp historians, put it:

'Every month during the 20s, 30s, and 40s, millions of red-blooded American males barricaded themselves behind the bathroom doors of the nation with the latest

ABOVE

Illustrators for the Penny Dreadfuls, *such as 'Varney the Vampyre; or, The Feast of Blood,' never signed their work. (1847) (See page 17)*

OPPOSITE

No credit was given to the artists who illustrated the hundreds of front covers of Nick Carter Weekly. *(March, 1904) (See page 18)*

offerings of their favorite pulp magazine. Proscribed by parents, condemned by educators, and ignored by critics, the pulps were the development of a fiction form rooted in the early 19th century, and were, according to the magazine *Playboy*, "those likable lurid novels for which whole forests were levelled and upon which a whole generation of American youth was hair-raised."'

The pulps were the young men's magazines of their time – a period of time in the U.S. that was more puritanical, more troubled, and more repressed than it is initially possible to believe of a nation that so prides itself on its freedoms. Some women did read these magazines – the columns of readers' letters in quite a few provide evidence of an open-minded minority who wanted more equality with the men in their lives – but the rights that women enjoy today were a long way off.

It has been said that the pulps, with their bluntly provocative titles and lurid covers, were a 'cradle of sensationalism.' But that ignores the fact that they were the medium through which some excellent and sometimes experimental writing was published. They were also the place where some memorable art appeared, as the pages of this book will bear convincing witness. Although the magazines were mass-produced and largely stereotyped in their genres, they were read as eagerly then as television programmes are watched by people today. The constant need to fill pages, month after month, gave the more adventurous editors and art directors the excuse to publish whatever took their fancy, and they were safe in the knowledge that they could lay their hands on plenty of more traditional fare for any nit-picking readers who complained.

It is important to know a little of the history of those times in order to put the magazines into the context of the events that shaped the major genres that are the focus of this book. In January 1920, for instance, the Eighteenth Amendment to the U.S. Constitution came into force, banning the production and sale of alcohol. Prohibition had, of course, been operating in some states since the middle of the previous century, because alcohol was viewed there as a sin and a lot of married women were convinced that bars would ruin family life. Only the mayor of New York foresaw the biggest problem – he reckoned he would need an extra 250,000 police officers to keep the city dry. Indeed, the harder the authorities

NEW NICK CARTER WEEKLY

Issued Weekly   By Subscription $2.50 per year.   Entered as Second Class Matter at New York Post Office by STREET & SMITH, 238 William St., N. Y.

No. 375.   Price, Five Cents.

THE DEVIL WORSHIPERS
OR THE DEFIANCE OF DAZAAR

BY
THE AUTHOR OF
"NICK CARTER"

The gigantic Thibetans sprang into the hallway from the parlor door. Nick Carter was prepared for the attack,
and dealt the first one a terrific blow with the butt of his weapon.

One group of churchmen was so incensed by the playing of jazz that they described it as 'a return to the jungle.'

tried, the harder the people, especially the young, rebelled. Scott Fitzgerald chronicled as much in his novels, such as *This Side of Paradise* (1920), in which he caught the spirit of fast-living youth and coined the term 'The Jazz Age.'

In the world of fashion, too, skirts were getting higher and higher, in a trend toward 'minimum clothes and maximum cosmetics,' as one writer described these 'shocking' sights. Corsets were also on the way out and sexy underwear was very much in – although in a handful of states the authorities became so alarmed about this that they seriously suggested that 'inappropriately dressed women' should be locked up. Along with drinking, which took place surreptitiously, of course, and at a quarter a shot was an expensive pursuit, smoking was frowned upon, as well as shaking about to the latest dance crazes, especially the Charleston. One group of churchmen was so incensed by the playing of jazz that they described it as 'a return to the jungle,' and in 1927 the blonde bombshell Mae West pushed the boundaries of propriety even further with her play *Sex*, which mocked the conventions of virtue and decency. Evidence was given against her by some police officers who sneaked into a performance, and Mae was found guilty of indecent behavior, fined $500, and sent to prison for 10 days. The sexual revolution had arrived, even if it was not yet quite under way.

On the other hand, crime and gangsterism were growing worse as the

decade progressed – culminating in the infamous Valentine's Day Massacre in Chicago on February 14, 1929, when seven mobsters were lined up against a beerhouse wall and mown down with sub-machine guns. The killers were all in the employ of Al Capone and were 'protecting' his monopoly in the city in the supplying of boot-leg liquor, extortion, and prostitution. Worse still was to come on October 24, 1929, when Wall Street crashed and 13 million shares were traded on a panic-stricken New York stock exchange. This 'Black Thursday' marked the start of the Depression, which would affect the whole of the U.S. during the next few years. It would take the steadying hand of the new president, Franklin D. Roosevelt, to put the country back to work, end Prohibition (in 1933), and wage war against organized crime. For most folk there was little relief from this gloom apart from the escapism of radio, the movies, where the 'talkies' had just arrived, and, as it transpired, the pulps – tickets to cheap thrills and gaudy pictures for the price of small change. Few publishing phenomena were better timed than that of the pulp magazines.

The pulp magazine was the idea of a former telegraph operator from Augusta, Maine, named Frank Andrew Munsey. He came to New York in 1882 determined to become a publisher. He had a simple maxim, 'The story is more important than the paper it is printed on,' and he knew that, thanks to the advent of the new high-speed printing presses, it was possible to mass-produce

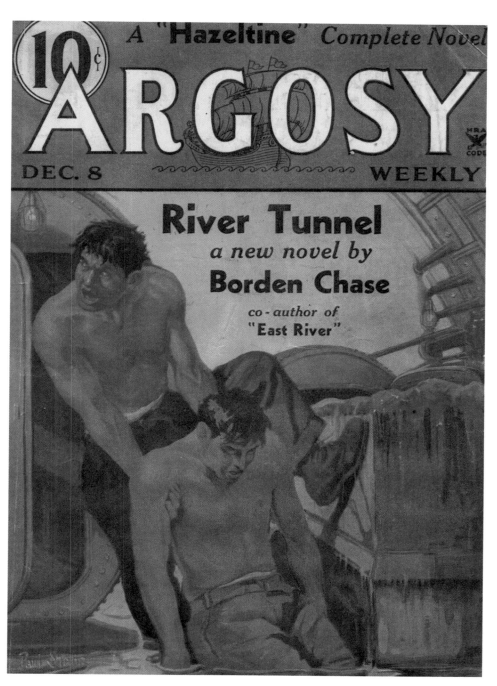

ABOVE

The versatile Paul Stahr provided many gritty, dramatic covers for Argosy. *(December, 1935) (See page 18)*

magazines in a way that had never been possible before. Munsey was well aware that the other popular publications of the time, such as *Harper's*, *Scribner's*, and *The Century* were printed on glossy or 'slick' paper made of rag-content stock. But he decided that if he used the much cheaper pulp paper, which was derived from a wood-fiber base and referred to as 'newsprint,' he would be able to offer a much cheaper product. He would give readers a suggestion of value for money by giving the magazines a four-color cover printed on art paper. The saving in costs, Munsey reckoned, would enable him to sell his 'pulps' at 10 cents – less than half the price of a typical slick. It was a decision that would make his fortune and revolutionize publishing.

The resulting pulp magazines measured, on average, 10 by 7 inches. The number of pages was normally 128 – containing something like 120,000 words of fiction – all stapled together through the cover, close to the spine. The paper, on which the text was printed in double columns, was thick and porous, and the edges were left uncut. The magazines gave off an unmistakable smell, which is still detectable in surviving copies today, and the pages usually turned yellow within months. But such factors failed to discourage the millions of potential readers who earned only meager wages. The average earnings of a factory hand, for example, were about $7 for a 10- to 12-hour day. Such people just wanted entertainment and escapist fare: simple, fast, and graphically illustrated.

RIGHT

Many of Adventure's *action-packed covers were the work of Hubert Rogers. (October, 1937) (See page 20)*

The pulps came into being as rivals to the slicks, which catered to the better-off sections of the U.S., and they quickly earned a reputation for being exploitative, unsophisticated, violent, and sexist. While this was to a degree true, they were also the proving grounds in which some great writers first made their mark – men such as Edgar Rice Burroughs, Max Brand, Zane Grey, Dashiell Hammett, Raymond Chandler, Erle Stanley Gardner, Howard Phillips Lovecraft, Clark Ashton Smith, Abraham Merritt, Robert E. Howard, Robert E. Heinlein, John D. MacDonald, Isaac Asimov, Ray Bradbury, and many others whose names will crop up in these pages. As more than one historian of the era has noted, there has not been a time, before or since, when so much entertaining fiction was available to so many so cheaply – albeit with a fair helping of trash thrown in, too.

The quality of the cover art and interior illustrations of the pulps has similarly been unfairly ridiculed without due study being made. In the early days, there were generally very few pictures inside the magazines, and those that there were had to be drawn in simple, bold strokes to avoid being over-inked or smudged into unrecognizable blurs when printed on the pulp paper. With the passage of time, however, a whole school of artists, some now deservedly famous and others long overdue for recognition, provided colorful, action-packed pictures of every conceivable situation, all intended to part customers from their hard-earned cash. At its best, the artwork had the same come-on effect as contemporary graphic art elsewhere, such as a poster advertising a new feature film or the next episode of a serial. These pictures may not always have been an accurate reflection of the contents, but their impact on sales was undeniable. Writing about this element of pulp magazine history in his *Handbook of American Culture* (1977), Bill Blackbeard has said:

'Illustrating the pulps was nearly as important for sales in the 1930s as the lurid covers of nickel thrillers had been for their prosperity at the turn of the century ... Supplying the considerable quantity of artwork was the task of a few dozen well-worked, professional ink, watercolor, and oil artists, who

The pulps quickly earned a reputation for being exploitative, unsophisticated, violent, and sexist.

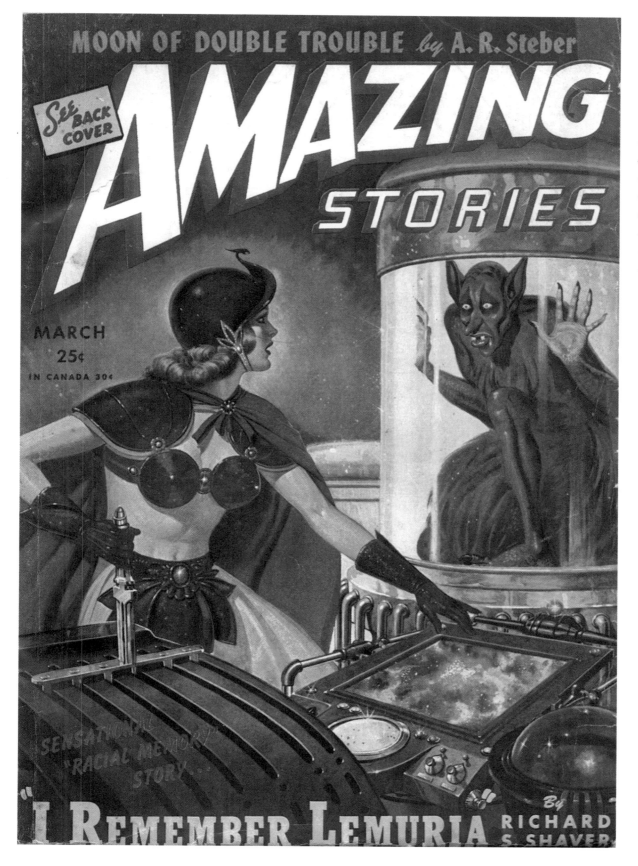

(See page 20)

LEFT
Robert Gibson Jones never lacked ingenuity when illustrating the covers of Amazing Stories. (March, 1945)

A gloriously colorful era packed with compelling – occasionally notorious – images

varied in quality and reputation from the dreariest kind of scrawlers and daubers who worked for Desperation Row (as the skin-of-their-teeth pulp houses were called) to a number of fine artists of international fame who did occasional or regular pulp magazine illustrations for bread-and-butter money. Most, of course, were artists of reasonable competence and occasional flairs of real genius.'

Among the roll call of these artists are names such as Paul Stahr, Hubert Rogers, John Newton Howitt, Walter M. Baumhofer, Max Plaisted, Harold S. DeLay, Earle Bergey, Peter Driben, Enoch Bolles, Amos Sewell, Tom Greiner, Hans Waldemar Wessolowski, Howard V. Brown, Fred Craft, Rudolph Belarski, Rafael De Soto, Tom Lovell, Norman Saunders, J. E. Allen, Lyman Anderson, H. V. Parkhurst, Rudolph W. Zirm, Frank R. Paul, H. J. Ward, Monroe Eisenberg, Marvin Singer, Robert Gibson Jones, Virgil Finlay, Peter Poulton, Alexander Leydenfrost, Paul Orban, John Fleming Gould, Hannes Bok, Leo Morey, Alex Schomberg, Wynne W. Davis, Edd Cartier, Frank Kelly Freas, not

forgetting a trio of outstanding women, Margaret Brundage, Irene Zimmerman, and Pauline Drappier. It is the artists' work that is especially being celebrated in this book. Without it the pulps might have amounted to only a chapter or two in publishing history rather than a gloriously colorful era packed with compelling – occasionally notorious – images that today provoke feelings of nostalgia among those old enough to remember, and a nod of admiration from younger generations seeing them for the first time.

It has to be admitted that there were cheap publications for the masses long before Frank Munsey initiated the 'rag-paper to pulp-riches' era from his offices at 280 Broadway, in New York. Almost a century earlier, a London entrepreneur, Edward Lloyd, had been at the forefront of a group of publishers in the city issuing *Penny Dreadfuls*, which enthralled the British public with serial stories of action, adventure, and plenty of lust (nothing new, you see). 'Varney the Vampyre; or, The Feast of Blood' (1847), the daring exploits of 'The Smuggler King' (1849), and the semi-pornographic liaisons of 'The Merry Wives of London' (1850) all had

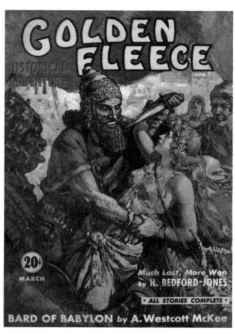

ABOVE

Historical subjects were a speciality of Harold S. DeLay, who worked for a number of the pulps, notably Golden Fleece. *(March, 1939)* *(See page 20)*

OPPOSITE

The unmistakable Virgil Finlay frequently combined action, adventure, and sex appeal in his covers for Famous Fantastic Mysteries. *(July, 1942)* *(See page 20)*

The artist who painted this gorgeous nude cover for the October 1933 issue of Stolen Sweets *has never been identified. (See page 20)*

ABOVE

Illustrations such as this one, of a beautiful African girl on the cover of Tattle Tales, *were extremely rare in the pulps. No artist is credited. (July, 1933)*

lurid front-cover illustrations of gory encounters and terrified maidens. A little later, the firm of Beadle and Adams was the first to catch the U.S. public's fancy with *Dime Novels*. These weekly publications recounted the exploits of men like the backwoods hero Deadwood Dick, the sporting champion Frank Merriwell, the ingenious boy inventor Frank Reade, and, perhaps most popular of all, the enduring young sleuth Nick Carter.

Frank Munsey launched the pulp era in 1896 with a short-story magazine of action and adventure tales, the *Argosy*. The magazine recruited its writers from everywhere – some, like Borden Chase, from the most unlikely backgrounds. Chase, whose real name was Frank Fowler, had worked in Chicago as a driver for Frankie Yale, a well-known bootlegger, until the day the mobster was shot by Al Capone. Fearing for his life, Fowler moved to New York, changed his name, and took to pulp writing with gusto. He remembered the experiences of those days well when he later moved again to Hollywood, where he soon became a script writer:

'I was like a lot of other guys who got into writing for the pulps because they were there. They were looking for people with imagination – it didn't matter if you hadn't been to some of the places you wrote about as long as you could tell a good story. The crime stuff came easy to me so that's what I did. The editors at Munsey's always needed copy fast and you could get a cheque as soon as the story was accepted and they signed a voucher. They paid a dollar a thousand words. I once heard a story that Frank Munsey would evaluate the worth of a story by how heavy the manuscript felt in his hand, but that never happened to me!'

The success of *Argosy* inspired several more titles, including *All Story Magazine, The Cavalier,* and *The Scrap Book,* all masterminded by Munsey's brilliant editor, Robert H. Davis – the man who discovered Edgar Rice Burroughs and Max Brand to name just two writers. Within a few years, the Munsey quarter had spawned an industry that would ultimately generate in excess of 300 titles. Their rivals were numerous, and all of them were anxious to get a piece of the pulp action: Street & Smith, Clayton Magazines, Popular Publications, Thrilling Publications, Culture Publications, the A. A. Wyn group, and many more who will all feature in the following pages. Although the pulps were sold predominantly in the U.S., some were exported to Europe

– often as ballast in merchant vessels – where they were sold off cheaply in chain stores like Woolworths. In time, Britain would produce its own range of pulps in what became known as the 'Mushroom Jungle.' The story of these 'Yankee Mags,' as they were called, is dealt with in the final chapter.

The variety of the pulps produced in the U.S. during their heyday was truly

ABOVE
The artwork of H. J. Ward came to typify the 'weird menace' pulps such as Spicy Mystery Stories. *(April, 1936) (See page 20)*

The artist who made Sheena, Queen of the Jungle, a pulp pin-up was another craftsman who was given no credit for his work. (Spring, 1951)

The Weird Story Magazine was one of the earliest pulps from Gerald G. Swan, the pioneer publisher of 'Yankee Magazines' in Britain. The cover artist signed himself 'Ron' and it has been suggested that the work may be that of Ron Embleton. (August, 1940)

incredible. Jostling alongside each other on the newsstands could be found *Adventure, Amazing Stories, Black Mask, Famous Fantastic Mysteries, Detective Story Magazine, Ghost Stories, Golden Fleece, Horror Stories, Marvel Science Stories, New York Nights, Oriental Stories, Private*

Detective, Spicy Mystery Stories, Stolen Sweets, Terror Tales, War Stories, and *Weird Tales* to name just a few. Also fighting for space were the solo titles *The Shadow, Doc Savage, Dusty Ayres and His Battle Birds, Secret Agent X, Doctor Death, Captain Satan, Sheena, Queen of the Jungle,* and a number of others that survived beyond the pulp era as paperbacks or comics, and have been fully dealt with elsewhere.

This list of titles merely hints at the dozens of similar magazines, catering for every possible taste, that poured from the presses in the U.S. during the years between the two world wars. Some would prove very successful. but others would disappear after only a single

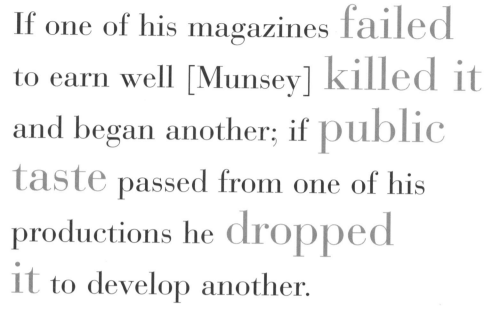

If one of his magazines failed to earn well [Munsey] killed it and began another; if public taste passed from one of his productions he dropped it to develop another.

ABOVE

Keyhole Detective Casebook *was a typical British pulp magazine, published in 1948 by Brown Watson. The illustration reversing the usual male/female situation is by Philip Mendoza.*

issue. The hard-nosed pulp magnates and quick-buck publishers who worked side-by-side in this pulp jungle were united only in one simple factor – their attitude toward every title they issued. If the public didn't buy it in sufficient quantities, they ceased its publication immediately. In this context, the *Dictionary of American Biography* has some rather unflattering things to say about the 'founding father,' Frank Munsey, which are no doubt just as true of many of his rivals:

'He was not a reformer, nor an idealist, nor was he deeply interested in any causes. His passion was to found or purchase magazines and, later, newspapers. If one of his magazines failed to earn well he killed it and began another; if public taste passed from one of his productions he dropped it to develop another.'

All the major pulp publishers were quick to seize on any new interest or trend, often following one another slavishly until the genre had become saturated with identical titles and sales dropped. It is perhaps pertinent to note that the rise of the superheroes like The Shadow, Doc Savage, Spider, and the others coincided with the downfall of public figures during the Depression. The rise of crime in the U.S. and the emergence of dictators in Europe were also regarded by the pulp publishers and their writers as forces that could be combated only by men of supernormal powers.

The pulps were not just intended to entertain the reader – they were also meant to make him feel better about himself, his prospects, and especially his sex life. With this in mind, companies did not use the magazines to sell ordinary things like clothes or food, but instead tried to sell any number of do-it-yourself fitness courses, cures for bad breath, sex aids, 'home' movies, quack medicines, peek-a-boo nighties, and – because the magazines were full of unclothed girls – even courses in learning how to draw. Charles Atlas, who offered to help scrawny young men to keep their girls, rather than lose them to sand-kicking bullies, was one of the most prolific advertisers. And several less reputable companies pandered to every fad and fancy imaginable in the magazine's personal columns at the back. On offer were 'unretouched' photographs of French models, methods for curing weak bladders, ruptures, and piles, potions and lotions to restore energy and 'pep,' instructions on how to hypnotize people (the illustration showing a beautiful girl, of course), pen pals for lonely hearts, and a whole range of illustrated booklets and novelties – 'The Kind Men Like!' And because this was the Depression, there were courses in how to become an electrician, a salesman, even a detective, plus any number of ways to 'Earn Money At Home!'

The eventual death knell for the pulps began to sound during and after the end of the Second World War. Paper fell into short supply and became more costly – as did the metal required for the staples. These became so expensive that some publishers were forced to use just one through the spine. Tastes were also changing. A new sophistication was evident among readers, and suddenly the pulps were being regarded as 'something from the old days.' On the literary scene, a whole new generation of writers was starting to emerge who aspired to more permanent – and better

paid – markets than the ephemeral, penny-a-line pulps. A few of the more popular pulp titles were down-sized to digest format by their proprietors, as if to deny their heritage. At the same time, the frantic pace of the storytelling disappeared, along with the unashamed gaudiness of the art, which had been essential ingredients of the pulps. As sales of the rest fell and the frequency of publication stumbled from monthly to quarterly, the major distributors servicing the nation's newsstands drove the final nail in the coffin by canceling their orders in favor of the exploding new market for comic books and original paperback fiction. Television, which was rapidly becoming a feature in every household, also cut savagely into the reading habits of the nation.

Ironically, at this very time, *Argosy* and *Blue Book*, which had pioneered the pulp legend, were revamped, and reappeared on the newsstands as slick magazines! Some people felt that Frank Munsey would have turned in his grave, but others believed that the old pulp-*meister* would have already acted before the writing was on the wall. Whatever the case, the pulp magazine legend was secure. But the telling of it has required the passage of time and an end to the prejudice and snobbery directed against a very special era – when cheap thrills and big shots were the stuff of dreams for millions of ordinary people.

OPPOSITE AND ABOVE LEFT AND RIGHT

These are three of the most popular types of advertisement to be found in the pulps during the 30s and 40s – although it was rare for the advertisers to go to the added expense of using color.

Snappy

25¢

1937

FALL EDITION

Illustrated·Fun And Fiction

All Undressed *and* Somewhere to Go

THE HOT PULPS

The year 1912 saw the tragedy of the sinking of the *Titanic* in the North Atlantic, a warning from a group of surgeons meeting in New York that taking cocaine could produce 'a race of fiends,' and the United States Modesty League declaring war on 'tight dresses.'

RIGHT

The illustrator Enoch Bolles was responsible for this beauty from a cover of Film Fun. *(See page 48)*

OPPOSITE

New babe for a new era – although the diaper pin and cigarette holder provided by the unknown artist for this issue of Snappy Stories *are strangely incongruous! (Fall, 1937)*

The same year also saw the publication of a new, mildly erotic magazine called *Snappy Stories*, by an enterprising publisher, William M. Clayton. He had sensed that the growing campaign by women for equal rights that was being fought on both sides of the Atlantic offered an unexpected opportunity where the U.S. prurient interest in love and sex was concerned. Already, women smoking in public were being labeled 'fast' – as were those who drank – so could sexual emancipation be far behind? William Clayton decided to seize the moment, and launched the first of what would in time become known as the 'hot' pulps.

Max Plaisted's style is easy to identify, as in this illustration for 'Love Has Wings' by Phyllis Hoerner in Snappy Stories. *(November, 1936)*

In their heyday, in the 30s, these magazines captured the mood of the times in the big cities with their night clubs and speakeasies, easy money, and easier morals. Their mixture of erotic fiction (mild by today's standards) and luscious artwork of sexy young girls proved a popular antidote to the general gloom of the Depression. Although primarily intended for male readers, the hot pulps also enjoyed a following among young girls, especially those who were – or dreamed of being – more uninhibited and daring like the flappers. Unlike the majority of other magazines, however, they were mostly sold as Under The Counter (U.T.C.) items at cigar stores, instead of on the newsstands. Their reputation for titillation – often far worse than it actually was – regularly earned them the close attention of the authorities at a time when the various state and local 'blue laws' were taking a hard line on sexual literature. Indeed, fans of the more notorious hot pulps – *Bedtime Stories*, *Scandals*, and *Stolen Sweets*, not forgetting the risqué worlds of *La Paree Stories* and *New York Nights* – often had

quite a search to lay their hands on the next issue after the police had been alerted by busybodies.

The magazines also developed a style all their own. The covers all carried brilliantly colored pictures of gorgeous young women, while inside, the pen-and-ink artists did their best to raise the temperatures of readers by picturing men and women in compromising situations. Despite the quality of this artwork, a substantial number of these illustrators did not sign their work, perhaps wanting to hide their identities. The indications are that some were artists of real talent who found work hard to come by during the Depression and were happy to take on any commissions going. Their artwork contributed in no small degree to the legend of the hot pulps, which some modern historians consider to be the original 'girlie magazines.' Certainly, their stock-in-trade of the female form unadorned (or as near as permissible), adds weight to this assertion, and they undeniably brought more than a little naughtiness into what were tough times for many people – not to mention sparking the fancies and fantasies of a generation.

William Clayton published *Snappy Stories* from premises on Lafayette Street in New York, slyly sub-titling it, 'Illustrated Fun and Fiction.' The covers initially featured artwork of pretty, if demure, young girls, but the twinkle in their eyes was intended to convey a message to readers that 'entertaining' was the keyword and that inside, amidst the gossip, poetry, and anecdotes intended to head off the authorities, would be found

Twice a Month
JULY 15, 1922
20 CENTS

Saucy Stories

WHAT A FOOL SHE HAD BEEN!
THE STRAIGHT AND NARROW
THE BOOB
BROADWAY LOVE
3. 4 WOMAN WHO WAS GOSSIPED ABOUT

ABOVE

Saucy Stories *was the biggest rival to* Snappy Stories, *and ran very similar tales of high living and low passions. The cover artist of this issue was David Arden. (July, 1922)*

some hot stories – by the standards of the times, admittedly. Subsequently, other publishers following Clayton's lead would employ similar codeword come-ons to get across the same message: 'peppy,' 'saucy,' 'spicy,' and so on.

The themes of the fiction in *Snappy Stories* generally fitted into one of three categories: single girls who became involved with the wrong kind of men (usually married and occasionally criminals); highly sexed women torn between marriage or adventure; and wives drawn into liaisons with other

men. At the conclusion, there was only one of three alternatives – the girls either overcame their emotions, gave way to their lust and paid the price (usually left fairly vague), or else were forgiven. Among those who regularly handled these stipulations for the magazines were Bertram Gordon ('Good Little, Bad Little Girl'), Ann Lawrence ('Husband Stealer'), and Malcolm Post ('A Little Bit Reckless'). The pulp also ran a 'Snappy Letter Box,' in which lonely readers sought pen pals and occasionally discussed their successes – take the example of a certain 'R. T.' of Boston who was warned, 'That's jail bait, Mister!' *Snappy Stories* also reviewed new books in 'Torrid Tomes,' and ran a column, 'Advice To Flappers,' in which Trixie Wolf dispensed wisdom on a variety of sexual topics, from the advisability of spending a weekend on a houseboat to whether girdles hampered romance. (Trixie considered them a 'downright menace – how would you like a pet dog with a steel jacket on?') One reader, signing herself 'Florine,' was even more forthright:

'My date last night insisted on unfastening the top of my stockings. He said he worked in a stocking factory and that I let my garters pull the hose too tightly. I thought maybe it was a gag, but gave him the benefit of the doubt. Did I do right or wrong?'

Trixie Wolf was very intrigued:

'It all depends on what you mean by that "doubt" you gave him the benefit

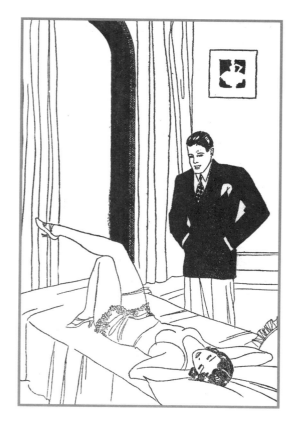

of: tell me more – I'm wild with curiosity. PS. Which type of unfastener was he? The Wild-Bull-in-a-China-Shop type ... or the gentle, artistic-hand type? Both have their advantages!'

Almost certainly, the best cover artist for *Snappy Stories* was E. K. Bergey, whose lithe-limbed beauties – sophisticated, cigarette-smoking city girls or beguiling rural charmers – attracted letters of admiration from many male readers. Earle Kulp Bergey was actually a skilled commercial artist who found his talent ideally suited to the pulps and drew for a number of magazines in different genres. He is especially fondly remembered by science fiction fans as the 'Inventor of the Brass Brassiere' because of the dozens of front covers he painted for *Startling Stories* of semi-naked girls coping with the vastness of space or the harshness of hostile planets dressed in little more than their underwear – albeit metallic. The pen-and-ink interior artwork was predominantly by Max Plaisted, another illustrator who is now best remembered for his work in the crime pulps.

Despite the success of *Snappy Stories*, which helped William Clayton to found a string of pulp titles, his empire encountered financial problems and in March 1933 went out of business. It was a sad end to the career of the man who had spiced up the nation with a little sexiness. However, his hot pulp survived, being taken over by B. T. Publishing, ostensibly based in Dover, the state capital of Delaware. The company actually maintained an editorial office in New York but, like a number of other such publishers, was clearly intent on keeping a low profile from the snoopers.

The biggest rival to *Snappy Stories* was *Saucy Stories*, the first issue of which appeared in 1915. It was created with 'the young, war-excited American in mind' by two New York editors, H. L. Mencken and George Jean Nathan, who were already partners in a 'Slick' magazine, *The Smart Set*. This rather snobby mix of gossip, advice, and 'high-class' fiction subtitled, 'A Magazine of Cleverness,' had been running for a couple of years and the two owners were looking to expand their business. In fact, it was easy enough for Mencken and Nathan to fill the new magazine with overmatter from *The Smart Set*, adding some specially commissioned risqué stories from their entourage of writers. In spite of this rather cynical policy, *Saucy Stories* matched the sales of its competitor for several years – and was noted for the rather languid but distinctive art of one of the few female pulp artists, Irene Zimmerman.

Two publications set the benchmark for this particular type of pulp, *Pep Stories* and *Spicy Stories*, which originated in 1922 – published, appropriately, on New York's 42nd Street, then, as today, enjoying a notoriety for cinemas, theaters, and

OPPOSITE
None of the accomplished artists who created the covers for Pep Stories *were given credit for their work. (October, 1929)*

TOP RIGHT
This picture by Irene Zimmerman teasingly illustrates 'Leave It to Bertie' by Clinton Harcourt for Saucy Stories. *(April, 1937)*

clubs trading in sex. 305 East 42 Street was the address of the King Publishing Company, the firm behind *Pep Stories* and *Spicy Stories*. Both pulps mixed columns of advice ('If You Would Woo' and 'Ask Me Anything') with humor ('The Spice of Life') and short stories with deliberately suggestive titles: 'Sneak Easily' by Gladys E. Dansfield ('Eve wasn't happy till she got herself in a tight corner with a married man'), 'But I Hardly Know You!' by Geoffrey Sayre ('Jim and Jill get jolly at a little celebration all their own'), and 'Some Girls Don't' by Frederick Carr, who was obviously one of King Publishing's star writers, if his amusing author blurb is anything to go by:

'The boys call him Fred and the ladies – "Oh, Freddy!" with a long drawn-out sigh after it. You and I know him as Frederick Carr and he's been writing for Spicy since we began. He works for a blue-nosed advertising concern during the eight-hour shift. He's supposed to write convincing copy on why you should wear Gordon's Bloomers instead of anybody else's, but Fred knows the ladies have switched to panties. Oh, yes, nice frilly ones in the loveliest pastel shades. So when the bloomer business gets too hot for him,

he sneaks home and writes us a good snappy story. In this way he keeps himself in trim for the job that pays him a living wage. One day, Fred got his stories mixed and the bloomer people were treated to a live-wire account of what "Fifi" did when the mailman rang the bell and Fifi was unprepared. They used about six tanks of oxygen and water trying to get the blue noses red!'

The artwork in both *Pep Stories* and *Spicy Stories* was always varied and interesting. Tom Arden was responsible for the vast majority of the cover girls, whom he painted in many unlikely situations – one petite, darkhaired beauty was poised on a weighing machine and another hung by a single leg from a crane hook, while inside, the unsigned line drawings were as likely to be bedroom scenes as artists' models posing. All this exciting female flesh put the writers on their mettle, and contributors to *Spicy Stories* in particular were never short of a colorful turn of phrase when it came to describing the female anatomy, breasts in particular.

'*The girl's breasts appeared determined to break through their scant covering.*'

'*She had perfect globes rampant upon a field sublime crowned by bright pink nipples, crinkly crisp.*'

'*Her breasts were like two beautiful bombs, ready to explode with allurement under the tight dress.*'

There was much more about '*the dimpled allure of magnificent breasts,*' '*plenteous silky-white mounds,*' and '*bulging, creamy hillocks*' as well as the occasional more risqué turn of phrase:

'*Mary had hips that were slimly rounded and formed a fitting counterpart to the saucily cerise-tipped breasts that sprouted girlishly.*'

'*She slipped her peach-colored panties down her smooth thighs thus giving a close-up of downy nooks and delicious contours.*'

But despite all this foreplay, the *Spicy Stories* writers never quite delivered, as the following typical extract from Geoffrey Sayre's 'But I Hardly Know You' demonstrates.

'*Jill wriggled out of her dress, then kicked off her slippers. With deft fingers*

Spicy STORIES

SEPTEMBER
25¢

A New Novel
by
C. S. Montanye
"Some
Girls
Don't"

SELF-
SUPPORTING

ABOVE
The frequent tales about artists' models in Spicy Stories *gave the illustrators plenty of scope for nudity. This example appeared in 'Afternoon Adventure' by Maureen Ahern. (July, 1932)*

LEFT
Tom Arden was a master at putting lithe young beauties into unlikely situations for the covers of Spicy Stories. *(September, 1931)*

ABOVE
Caught in the act! This was a familiar situation for illustrators to depict in La Paree Stories. *(September, 1933)*

OPPOSITE
Peter Driben developed his talent in magazines such as La Paree Stories *to become one of the finest painters of the female form. (March, 1933)*

she peeled off her stockings. The light of a street lamp outside gleamed faintly on the snowy flesh of her shoulders, her throat. Nonchalantly, while Jim's temples throbbed feverishly, she tossed aside her brassiere, then, after a second's hesitation, she slipped out of the silk pretty that caressed her. And Jim, looking on avidly, missed not a detail of her charms.

'Suddenly standing erect, Jill cast a frightened look about. 'Good heavens, I left my nighties in the other room. Oh, what'll I do – what'll I do?' It was too much for Jim. Leaping over to her, he exclaimed: 'I only met you today, but since that son of Italy locked us in here, I feel as though I've known you for years.' 'Well, there's something to that,' said Jill, pulling his head down so her lips would not remain unoccupied.

'And since, snappy readers, we really are hardly acquainted with them, perhaps this is the proper moment to leave them alone.'

Pep also teased its readers, in much the same way, while still raising all their expectations:

'No matter where you go today, or what you do, or what you say – it's got to be snappy and full of speed; right up to the minute and no lagging behind. We're a fast crowd today and we do not tolerate slow ones. Peppy stories, a flock of jokes and flashy illustrations for your particular taste. That's why we say: Get snappy – join the crowd – read *PEP*!'

Pep and *Spicy Stories* also set a trend in advertising sex-orientated goods. Alongside the ubiquitous ads for muscle-building and making money were special offers of books such as *A Healthy Sex Life & How To Achieve It* by A. J. Wolbarst M.D., *The Secrets of Sex Attraction* by French Roy, and the anonymous *Padlocks and Girdles of Chastity*, plus cut-price introductions to 'French Love Drops' (Essence of Ecstasy), 'Glow of Life' (Helps You Overcome Your Sexual Weaknesses), and 'French Hot Bedroom Poses.' Fully appreciating that there would be women reading the magazines, advertisers also offered 'New, Easy Ways to Feminine Hygiene,' 'Werco French Tonic Tablets,' and 'Bust Developers – Add 1 to 3 Inches in 30 Days.'

If there was an obvious French influence in a lot of this advertising, it was not altogether surprising. For years, Americans, many of whom had had their first experience of Paris during the Great War, had nursed a great affection for France, its history, its love of

MARCH
25 Cents

La Paree STORIES

NRA

**Bird of
Paradise**
By Henri Lamoreaux

'It is quite likely that Renee would have brought their desire to a deliciously successful conclusion right then and there.'

independence, and especially what was regarded as its 'invention' of the art of *l'amour*. All French women were considered beautiful and sexually liberated, the men handsome and skilled at lovemaking, while Paris was the undisputed capital of love. Small wonder, then, that several enterprising pulp publishers climbed aboard the bandwagon for hot magazines by copying the most famous of French magazines, *La Vie Parisienne* – the world's first publication to discuss and illustrate the joys of *l'amour*.

Since 1863, *La Vie Parisienne* had been delighting its readers with superb illustrations of females in every stage of dishabille from a glimpse of stocking to total nudity. Many of these beauties were in the process of bathing or going to bed when surprised by amorous suitors. This formula was first copied in the pulps by *La Paree Stories* from the Merwil Publishing Company founded by two brothers from the West side of New York in 1928. The fact that none of the writers or artists used by Merwil had ever been to Paris is evident from even the most cursory glance at *La Paree Stories*, but this did nothing to prevent the magazine from being an immediate success. The titles of the stories and the authors' 'names' were calculated to grab the attention of lonely American males dreaming of sexually

voracious women. 'The Flaming Torch' by Henry Lamoreaux in one early issue contained the archetypal U.S. view of the French *femme fatale*:

'Renee's mouth was the more aggressive of the two, and Paul's lips felt as though they were being subjected to a powerful suction pump. His response left nothing to be desired, and if Renee's friend, Marie, had not laughed excitedly just before she popped back into the room, it is quite likely that Renee would have brought their desires to a deliriously successful conclusion right then and there.'

La Paree Stories was the first magazine to publish cover art by the talented Peter Driben. His voluptuous Gallic maidens guaranteed sales, although his drawings of French men tended to conform to the stereotypical ideal, with arched eyebrows, waxed

moustache, and drooling lips. Driben's art for *La Paree Stories*, along with his later work for several other hot pulps, is now very popular with collectors.

The fiction in *La Paree Stories* featured an unending procession of models, dancers, gamblers, roues, and nymphomaniacs. Most of them talked in the most excruciating pidgin French, peppered with phrases similar to 'Mon Dieu,' 'Mon amour!' and 'Mai oui, cherie.' Flirtation was the name of everyone's game and, though the women seemed ready to cast off their clothing after the briefest of introductions, the sex act tended to occur behind closed doors or in a flurry of asterisks.

The magazine's letters page, 'Tete-a-tete,' made for interesting reading, too. One man signing himself 'H. K. P.' of Illinois hinted that in his case at least the magazine was for more than just reading or looking at:

NEW YORK NIGHTS

35^c

NUMBER 4

'*La Paree* comes the nearest to being a perfect companion for an evening alone on those occasions when a man would really prefer not to be alone. When he is not alone, the magazine is the only acceptable third party. Then it completes the perfect trio.'

Another writer, 'R. W. R.' from Ohio, also enthused,

'The illustrations are great, but why not give them a little more life and take a little more off?'

But the prize surely went to a female reader signing herself 'A. K.' of New York, who complained in March 1933,

'If you must compromise on the pictures, your pen-and-ink artists can surely at least show that the men are interested – you know what I mean.'

The frank Miss A. K. was not done there, either.

'Here are some more suggestions. (1) Enlarge your mailbag section. (2) Get letters from spanked and spankers of both sexes. It isn't only the girls that get spanked. One of the girls here spanked her boyfriend the other night. She'd love to tell you about it. It was interesting, too. I was watching,

LEFT

'"*I'm ready to gobble up lovely adventurous girls,*" *he said.* "*Coming?*"' *This suggestive caption in* 'She Couldn't Say Don't' *by Ray King in* New York Nights! *was typical. (July, 1934)*

ABOVE

This is an example of Peter Driben's work for New York Nights. *(May, 1934)*

ABOVE

'Afternoon Adventure' by Maureen Ahern in Spicy Stories. *(September, 1931)*

RIGHT

The artist who drew this inviting little beauty for French Night Life Stories *was probably Peter Driben. (August, 1934)*

though he didn't know. (3) Letters on the art of petting. Give the girls a chance here, too. If my boyfriend writes about my milky white thighs and the brevity, flimsiness, and spaciousness of my step-ins, you would publish it. Give me a chance to tell you what interests me!'

The success of *La Paree* encouraged Merwil to launch *New York Nights*, which featured the same kind of steamy passion – but much closer to home. Peter Driben again drew the covers, and a group of anonymous pen-and-ink men did their best for stories like 'She Couldn't Say Don't' by Ray King, 'She Would Be Wooed!' by Zita Romaine, and the delightful 'You Can Never Trust Elastic' by Atwater Culpepper. On occasions, the slush-pile of manuscripts for *La Paree* must have come in handy for its companion, if tales such as 'Paris – Ah, Paris!' by Tom Kane and 'Plastered in Paris' by Carol Gable are anything to go by.

The first major competitor to *La Paree Stories* came from just a few blocks away at 115 West 27th Street, where H. M. Publishing launched *French Night Life Stories* in 1930. The company invested in top-quality artwork for the covers, but rather spoiled the effect inside by using an artist named Melger whose work resembled the cartoon character, Betty Boop. It certainly did nothing to enhance stories pulsating with emotion like 'Angelic Angelique' by Abelard Trello and 'Caresses For The Countess' by Ray King. *French Frolics*, which came from the same company a year

...unknown artists... provided excellent nudes in a variety of exotic poses for the covers...

later, was better served by the unknown artists who provided excellent nudes in a variety of exotic poses for the covers, while the fiction, especially tales by the prolific Charles B. McCray, such as 'All Undressed and Some Place to Go,' was of a generally higher standard.

The best of the French-inspired hot magazines was undoubtedly *Paris Nights*, which was launched in 1931 by

ABOVE LEFT

This revealing nude appeared on the cover of French Frolics. *The added hint of bondage would have confined this issue to U.T.C. sales. (January, 1934)*

ABOVE RIGHT

Tom Greiner drew this winsome lovely for Paris Nights. *(August, 1933)*

'To Hinky's stricken eyes, vibrant life seemed to emanate from every curve and undulation of her throbbing body.'

ABOVE
A typical piece of artwork by the prolific Ward Story for Paris Nights. (December, 1933)

the Shade Publishing Company, at 1008 West York Street in Philadelphia. The magazine ran for longer than any of its rivals and has since become very collectable because of the unmistakable artwork of Tom Greiner, whose beautiful young girls may often have looked more homegrown than French, but were still perfect pinup material. The magazine also ran a monthly photo art section temptingly referred to on the cover as 'Featuring Dainty, Shapely Art Models.'

The publishers made no attempt in *Paris Nights* to pretend that any of the fiction was the work of French authors, and among the magazine's contributors were several already prolific pulp writers including Derek Bechdolt ('A Man in Her Bedroom'), Dorothy Quick ('Love For Art's Sake'), and Jackson M. Hall, whose steamy little tale of 'Getting Even With The Count' contained a scene that came straight out of every young man's fantasy:

'The Mediterranean moonlight bathed everything in a gauzy, ghostly sheen. Hinky swung himself onto the gallery – and stopped. An open window yawned upon the balcony and through it the startled Hinky viewed a naked figure of vivid, pulsing, devastating beauty, swathed in moonbeams. On a bed in the moonlit chamber lay a woman alone. To Hinky's stricken eyes, vibrant life seemed to emanate from every curve and undulation of her throbbing body. Her head drooped backward, her ruby lips were parted, her eyes were closed and her rippling, Titian hair cascaded down upon her heaving, pink-tipped breasts, in a pool of beauty. Hinky's breathing accelerated into swift, ardent gasps. It was with an exertion of will that he restrained himself from leaping in through the window.

'Her whole body appeared burnished as with gold – as though it were but itself a rapturous part of those

LEFT
An artist known only by the signature 'Jas' illustrated hundreds of racy yarns for Paris Nights and several of the other hot pulps. This is an illustration for the story 'Getting Even With The Count' by Jackson M. Hall. (November, 1933)

OPPOSITE
Tom Greiner was the cover artist for Shade Publishing's Paris Gayety. (March, 1934) (See page 41)

PARIS GAYETY

SNAPPY, MIRTHFUL STORIES AND WORLDLY PASTIMES

25¢ MARCH

NRA

PRIM BUT PRIMITIVE

By

Kirk Wolff

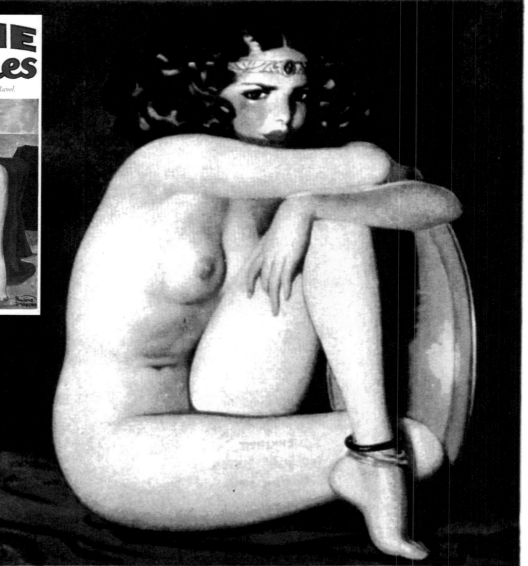

ABOVE

The distinctive style of Pauline Drappier was seen on many covers of Bedtime Stories. *(March, 1935)*

RIGHT

This bewitching painting of Salome was one of a series of nude portraits of famous women that have made Bedtime Stories *very collectable. (July, 1933)*

'His mission here was to procure that golden screw, and he was a man with a purpose...'

"Shall we see how they fit?"
Phil asked.

delicate lunar shafts, destined to vanish as would the moonbeams with the first obscuring cloud. But Hinky was his own man. With a tremendous effort of will, he tore away his enraptured gaze, skulked across the gallery, insulating his aroused body in the protective shadows, and gained the Count's window. His mission here was to procure that golden screw, and he was a man with a purpose...'

The magazine also ran cartoons and two regular columns, 'Parisian Paragraphs' and 'Boudoir Chatter – Our Department of the Interior Where, Behind Closed Doors and Drawn Curtains, We Amuse Ourselves with Idle Chatter of the World and its Follies.' *Paris Nights* featured the unusual pen-and-ink artwork of Ward Story who was at his best when illustrating saucy ditties, and a prolific artist known only as 'Jas,' whose rather naive style is to be found in various pulp magazines of the period and is immediately recognizable for the correctness of male attire and the almost total lack of any on his languid women. In 1933, Shade Publishing issued a companion magazine, *Paris Gayety*, which utilized the same stable of writers and artists.

The seductive *Bedtime Stories*, which appeared that same year, was another title from B. T. Publishing. Flushed with the success it was enjoying with *Snappy Stories*, after taking it over from Clayton, B.T. decided to take the hot formula a step further. Fiction like Max Markon's 'In The Middle of the Night,' Cliff Carruth's 'Great Lover,' and the remarkably explicit 'Pleasure Mad' by Grace Holmes was coupled with a regular column, 'Boudoir Chatter,' and promotions for a line of special 'home' movies. A female artist, Pauline Drappier, produced a number of the covers, while inside there was more

ABOVE LEFT
Suggestive captions were a feature of
Bedtime Stories. *This example – '"Shall we see how they fit?" Phil asked' – is from 'Two Grand' by Malcolm Post. (April, 1937)*

work by Jas, and the occasional appearance of work by the portrait painter Robert Linton, who signed himself with the single letter 'R.' Another obviously talented artist, he was even more reluctant to reveal his connection with *Bedtime Stories*, but provided the magazine with a series of sensational covers in 1933 featuring some of the most beautiful women in

in Springfield, Massachusetts, but maintained an editorial and advertising office on East 42nd Street in New York. The covers of *Scandals*, which carried the message 'Stories of people like those you know' (readers no doubt hoped) were painted anonymously. But inside could be found the highly individualistic Gallic styles of Jehan Testevuide, Alain Fadul, Rene Giffey, and Daniel

D.R.'s pictures of women in the privacy of their apartments were heavy with undertones of sexuality and occasionally lesbianism.

history, including the tempting Madame Du Barry, the haughty Cleopatra, and the utterly bewitching Salome, all virtually naked. The issues with these covers are now among the most valuable of all pulps.

High-quality, exotic artwork that had been purchased from several French magazines was a particular attraction in another of the 30s' hot magazines *Scandals*. It was produced by Delo Publications, which gave its address as 29 Worthington Street

Ronpierre, who signed himself 'D. R.' Ronpierre's pictures of women in the privacy of their apartments were heavy with undertones of sexuality and, occasionally, lesbianism.

Despite the French illustrations, the fiction in *Scandals* was unmistakably American, viz 'The Wah-Wah Girl' by James B. Wooding, 'The Fortunes of Frances,' by Patty Jeans, and Eileen Shannon's 'Where Men Are Men.' The magazine ran cartoons loaded with *double entendres* and a fortunetelling

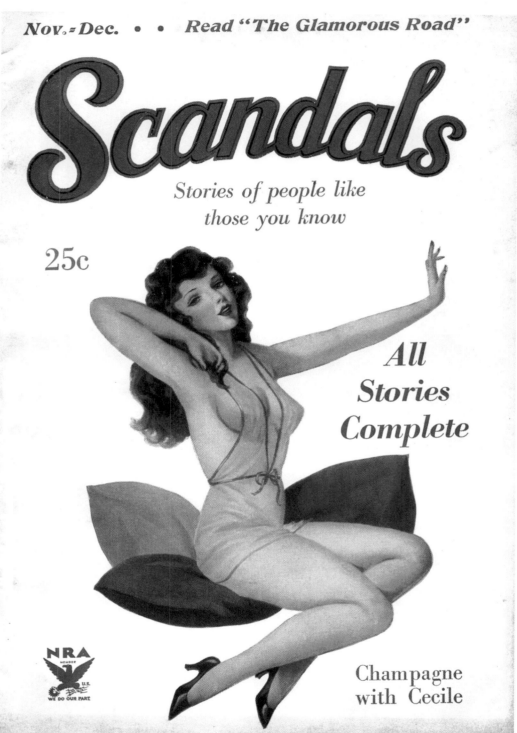

Nov.-Dec. • • *Read "The Glamorous Road"*

Scandals

Stories of people like those you know

25c

All Stories Complete

NRA MEMBER WE DO OUR PART

Champagne with Cecile

ABOVE

The work of a French magazine artist Daniel Ronpierre, with its undertones of female sexuality and lesbianism, was regularly featured in Scandals. *This picture illustrated 'How The Other Half Loves' by Virgie Cape. (October, 1934)*

ABOVE

Despite its penchant for revealing stories, Scandals never gave any details about its cover artists. (November/ December, 1934)

ABOVE

A touch of aerobics ahead of their time? The creator of this unique cover for Cupid's Capers *is unknown. (October, 1933)*

column, 'Love and Life,' which carried a subtitle, 'Probably No Other Force Is As Powerful in the Selection of Your Mate As Astrology.' Delo Publications later issued a companion pulp, *French Stories*, which shared many of the same writers and artists.

When it came to holding up a mirror to the tastes of young American males in the 30s – particularly their sexual fantasies – few of the hot pulps did it better than *Stolen Sweets* and *Cupid's Capers*, published in New York by the Edmar Publishing Company at 145 West 45th Street. *Stolen Sweets*, which appeared in 1933, offered readers a heady mixture of sex, money, and booze – the repeal of Prohibition had not yet taken place. Many of the stories featured night clubs, where business and crime went hand in hand and nice girls and call girls fell for the same line

of male chat. *Cupid's Capers* made its debut a few months later, prompting one reader to write to the editor:

'Congratulations, many of them, for bringing into the world *Cupid's Capers*, a great little companion to *Stolen Sweets*. For after all, Stolen Sweets are the result of Cupid's Capers, and the two of them just belong together. The art pictures in the nude were very beautiful – keep up the good work and bring on more of them!'

The covers of both magazines featured lush and erotic pinups, but the artists were never credited – neither were their talented compatriots inside, with the one exception of 'Hef' (presumably no relation of Hugh Hefner?), whose sketches were often wryly humorous. The two pulps ran

OPPOSITE

No artist's name is given for this portrait on the cover of Stolen Sweets *of a knowing young beauty in love with forbidden pleasures. (June, 1934)*

ABOVE RIGHT

An artist who signed himself 'Hef' created a series of illustrations for Cupid's Capers. *This one was for 'All In A Night's Stroll' by Roy Shannon. (February, 1934)*

Taking the plunge for entertainment, a cover by John Burley for Stage and Screen Stories. *(April, 1936)*

popular correspondence columns – 'Y Don't-cha Write Sometime?' in *Stolen Sweets* and 'Whang! Wow! Wham!' in the sister pulp – in which scarcely a letter from either sex did not appeal for a pen pal.

The bright lights of Broadway were a natural mecca for all those dreaming of a life of gaiety and fun – with a career as an actor or actress at the top of most people's wannabe list. On the West Coast, Hollywood similarly attracted the starry-eyed like a magnet, and the allure of both places was a natural subject for the hot pulps. Typical among these was *Stage and Screen Stories* published on Broadway – where else? – by Movie Digest Inc. Although it was described in its promotional material as 'Clean, spicy and wholesome,' it was a magazine that offered its readers stories like 'The Bathtub Lady' by Anita Delglyn ('The quick way to success is not always the best, as this extra girl found out'). It also featured Lars Anderson's yarns of John 'Satan' Devlin, a film company's cameraman, whose ability to satisfy a constant stream of

would-be young actresses was nothing short of amazing. John Burley illustrated many of the covers of *Stage and Screen Stories*, which had a tendency to concentrate on the glamor of Hollywood at the expense of the stage.

Saucy Movie Tales – subtitled 'Illustrated Snappy Fiction' – was also published by Movie Digest Inc. but concentrated solely on the film industry. The stories like 'Bright Lights' by Andre Sindos ('Two Blonde Venuses vie for Honors in Hollywood by Private and Public Appearances') and 'Such Is Hollywood' by Gloria Kent ('A Satiric

The girls of Stage and Screen Stories *were rarely anything other than scantily dressed. This is a scene from Anita Delglyn's tale of 'The Bathtub Lady.' (April, 1936)*

No matter what liberties a man might take with a woman, nothing would disturb his equilibrium – or his clothes! This illustration by Jack Lurie is for 'Cupid Captures Connie' from Saucy Movie Tales. (May, 1936)

ABOVE

The high life of Hollywood was a regular theme in Saucy Movie Tales, where the girls took off rather more than they put on. (March, 1936)

and Up-to-date Story of Hollywood by an Author who Knows Filmdom for What it Really is') were indeed well illustrated with an array of actresses and starlets who seemingly spent their entire lives, both on camera and off, in the skimpiest of underwear. The men, were forever taking liberties though they never removed so much as a tie.

Another pulp magazine, called *Film Fun*, which was published in Hollywood, devoted all its attentions to the film capital, and offered a mixture of gossip about the stars, plus some jokes and cartoons, and also short stories in which fun-loving, invariably naive girls from all over the U.S. almost fell into the clutches of the film world's worst lechers (usually ageing producers or directors) until the handsome young man of their dreams – a leading man, of course – stepped away from the camera to swear undying love. It was dreams made into fiction and, not surprisingly, the magazine was a great success during the 30s. Today, *Film Fun* is especially remembered for the wonderful covers painted by Enoch Bolles.

By the end of the decade, the hot magazines had all been chased off the scene by the law or closed by their owners – none, it has been claimed, ever

An array of actresses and starlets seemingly spent their entire lives in the skimpiest of underwear. The men were forever taking liberties, though they never removed so much as a tie.

failed financially, which says everything about their appeal. One or two, such as *Film Fun*, were transmogrified into pinup magazines packed with black-and-white photographs. Out went the steamy fiction and sexy illustrations and in came suggestive cartoons, blue jokes, and picture spreads of scantily clad show girls and starlets. The age of *Playboy* and *Penthouse* lay just around the corner in a more permissive society that these pulps had, in their way, helped to create.

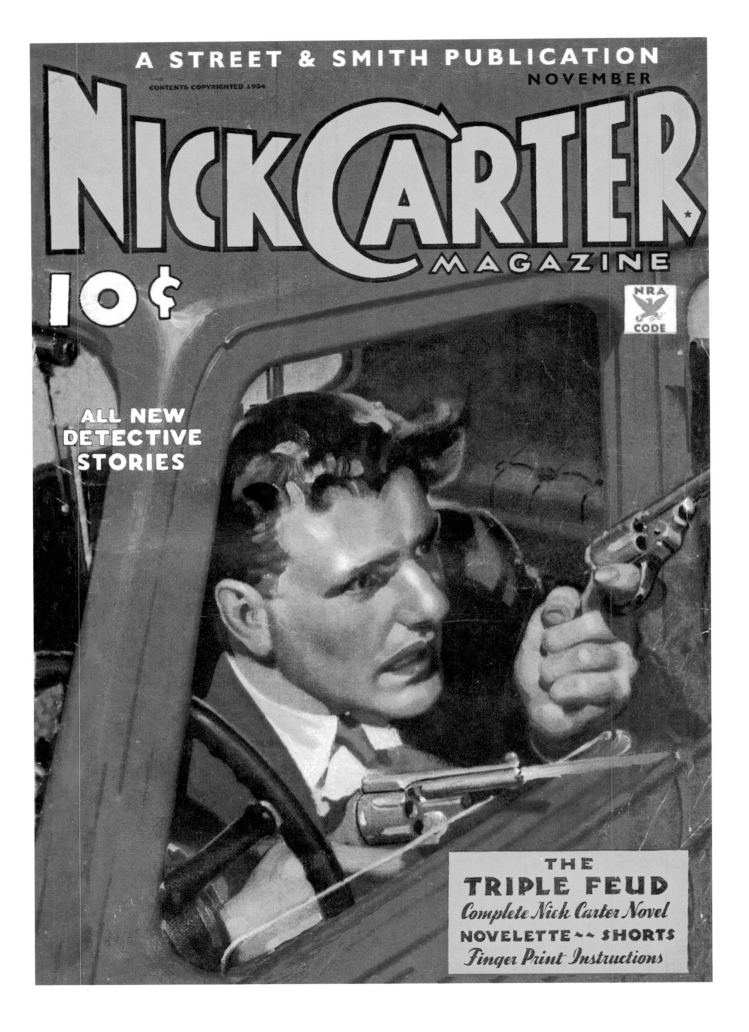

The Coming *of the* Hardboiled Dicks

THE CRIME PULPS

On a spring morning in the year 1915, Ormand G. Smith, son of one of the founders of the Street & Smith magazine publishing group, was sitting in his New York office overlooking Seventh Avenue, pondering over the sales figures of the company's many and varied periodicals.

RIGHT

This masked cracksman graced a cover of The Underworld Magazine. *(See page 77)*

OPPOSITE

This picture of the enduring detective of Nick Carter Magazine *was painted by Amos Sewell. (November, 1934)*

Among the magazines that were giving Smith concern was *Nick Carter Weekly*, the long-running saga of a young detective, whose adventures had begun in 1886. Ever since then, he had been battling a host of criminal archfiends and rescuing damsels in distress – as the titles on the front covers bear witness: e.g. 'Nick Carter From Peril to Peril,' 'Nick Carter and the Prince of Stranglers,' and 'Nick Carter and the Devil Worshippers.' It was evident from the start that a trend that would become still more apparent in the era of the pulps had

It was pretty young girls that evildoers invariably had it in for.

been clearly defined – it was pretty young girls that evildoers invariably had it in for.

Nick Carter was, however, a character of whom Ormond Smith was especially fond. For he had provided the original outline for the first story about the detective and handed it to one of his writers, John Russell Coryell, to develop. But notwithstanding this, something had to be done about the undeniable decline in Carter's fortunes, and Smith was not a man to shirk hard decisions. He called in his assistant Will Ralston and told him:

'People are getting tired of reading about the same characters week after week. They're even getting fed up with Nick Carter. Let's discontinue the *Nick Carter Weekly* and start a magazine that will have a dozen different detectives as characters. Perhaps some of them will catch on. We'll call it – oh – let's see ... What do you think of *Detective Story Magazine?*'

Although he could not have known it, on that day, the Street & Smith boss had made a decision that would influence the course of magazine publishing, and created the first pulp to be devoted entirely to crime fiction.

Fortunately for Nick Carter and his fans (some of whom, like the admirers of Sherlock Holmes, believed he actually existed), the detective did not die, but carried on to become the sleuth who has now appeared in more detective novels than any other character in U.S. literature – probably only the British detective Sexton Blake has solved more crimes. He also featured in his own pulp, the *Nick Carter Magazine*, in the 30s, in which he became a more raw-boned figure who could sometimes be less than gentlemanly to the fair sex; and later still, in the 60s, Carter metamorphosized into a sophisticated secret agent in paperback, and a star of films and television.

But that was all a long way in the future when Frank E. Blackwell, a former feature writer for the *New York Sun*, and recent employee of Street & Smith, was given the job of editing *Detective Story Magazine*. The first issue was published on October 17, 1915, with a cover by staff artist John A. Coughlin, who would later provide hundreds of covers and interior artworks for the magazine. There were detective stories by Nathan Day, Frank Parkes, Ross Beechman, R. Norman Grisewood, and Will R. Jones, plus the first episodes of two new serial stories:

OPPOSITE

John A. Coughlin illustrated this and many other covers of Detective Story Magazine. *(July 3, 1926)*

July 3, 1926

THERE'S ONLY ONE
DETECTIVE STORY MAGAZINE

15 Cents

Every ○ *Week*

Detective
Story Magazine

The Picaroon and the Pearls
By Herman Landon

'Brits of Headquarters' by Hilary Blake and 'The Yellow Label' – a story from the much-loved archives of Nick Carter. In a neat acknowledgment to the detective character who had been so influential in the creation of the magazine, Frank E. Blackwell credited the editorship of *Detective Story Magazine* to 'Nicholas Carter.'

Many of the stories in the new magazine were a far cry from the hardboiled yarns that would later come to typify the crime and detective pulps. Indeed, they almost harked back to the era of Sherlock Holmes, as can be judged by this text from 'Mr. Alias, Burglar' by Rodrigues Ottolengui from the June 1916 issue. The story features an amateur crime solver named Mr. Mitchell who, in this extract is addressing a crook and a bemused detective who has been summoned to hear about Mr. Mitchell's remarkable piece of detection:

"The affair is a little out of the ordinary," began Mr. Mitchell. "Mr. Alias called upon me two weeks ago and announced that he intended to commit a burglary. He offered to wager that I could not prevent him. I changed the word 'prevent' to 'detect' and took the wager. I also asked for two weeks instead of one, as he had first suggested. I win the wager because I can explain every detail of the robbery which occurred last night when Mr. Alias came into this room and abstracted a diamond from my desk. Moreover, he has the property in his pocket now and I will thank him to restore it!"

Many of the stories ... were a far cry from the hardboiled yarns that would later come to typify the crime and detective pulps.

Detective Story Magazine sold for 10 cents and was initially published twice a month. Such was its success, that the following year Ormond Smith decided it should be released weekly – and so it continued until well into the 30s, when it returned to twice monthly for the rest of its publishing life. In his history of Street & Smith, *The Fiction Factory* (1955), Quentin Reynolds has this to say about the magazine:

'After it became a weekly, it was off on one of the most sensational and enduring careers any magazine in the country ever enjoyed. It would thrive and lead the field of detective fiction for 30 years. Its popularity was no accident, Blackwell corralled the best writers of detective fiction here and abroad. Their names were a roll-call of crime fiction.'

Indeed they were, and several of the writers whose work appeared in the pages of *Detective Story Magazine* would also feature in the pulp boom and go on to become internationally famous, including Max Brand, James Cain,

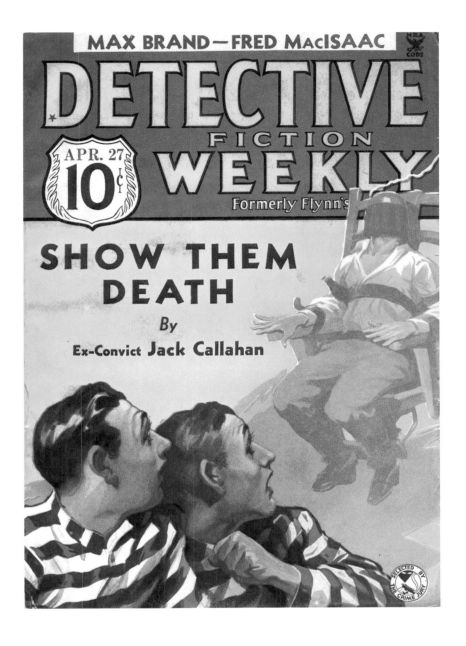

Detective Fiction Weekly *often had a 'message' on its cover, like this one with its powerful illustration of the electric chair by Joe Farer. (April, 1927)*

MacKinlay Kantor, and England's Edgar Wallace. A young artist named Amos Sewell, who produced some of his first work for Street & Smith, became a regular illustrator on the pages of the magazine and eventually handled both the covers and interior artwork for the *Nick Carter Magazine*. The lessons that he learned in Street & Smith's art department run by William 'Pop' Hines were to stand him in good stead, and his experiences were typical of what happened to many young artists in the hectic world of magazine publishing in the pulp era:

'Everyone wanted to work for Street & Smith,' Sewell recalled, 'because the established artists were there and getting good assignments and we could learn from them. Perhaps the experience was good for us – it was certainly a humbling experience. Pop Hines always had a wet palette in his office. We'd bring in our illustrations, and if he didn't like them he'd tell us to change them then and there.'

Despite Ormond Smith's remark that the public were tired of reading about the same character, the company enjoyed success with magazines featuring two great crime-fighters, The Shadow and Doc Savage, instalments of their adventures being published until the late 40s. In 1929, *Detective Story Magazine* was joined by a companion title, *Best Detective Stories*, which was made up of the pick of crime tales from all the Street & Smith publications. Both had dedicated readers until they ceased publication in 1949.

Two other crime pulps tried to challenge the success of *Detective Story Magazine*, but never succeeded in overhauling the sales of the original. The first was *Detective Fiction Weekly*, published by Frank A. Munsey's company, and the other *Clues*, subtitled 'A Magazine of Detective Stories,' which was issued by the Clayton Group.

Detective Fiction Weekly was a fairly unabashed copy of the Street & Smith pulp. It was launched in 1924 as *Flynn's* – named for the man who was ostensibly its editor, William J. Flynn, the former chief of the U.S. Secret Service. Flynn

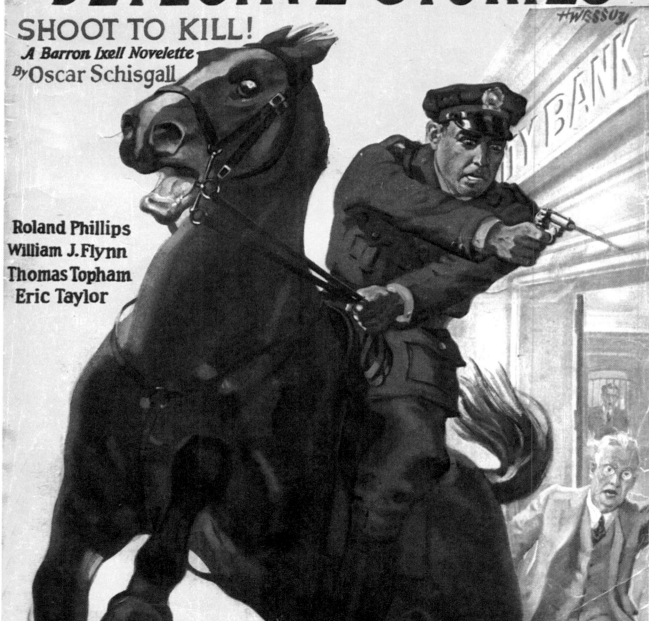

CLUES

20c

January, 1932

A Magazine of
DETECTIVE STORIES

SHOOT TO KILL!
A Barron Ixell Novelette
By Oscar Schisgall

Roland Phillips
William J. Flynn
Thomas Topham
Eric Taylor

A brash young lawyer named Barney Killigen was not a million miles removed from the great Perry Mason.

had written some fiction for *Argosy* in the 20s about Peabody Smith, 'a retired investigator for the Secret Service,' now taking on private assignments, and evidently based on the author's own experiences. The former chief built up a team of writers, including Anthony Wynne, Arthur B. Reeve, and Steve Fisher, who all continued to write after the name of the magazine was changed to *Detective Fiction Weekly* in 1928. The pulp then started running 'True Stories' like 'Show Them Death,' about life in prison, and 'Illustrated Crimes,' drawn by Paul Berdanier. A certain Major C. E. Russell contributed a regular column, 'The Criminologist Says,' while M. E. Ohaver gave advice on 'Solving Cipher Secrets.' Many of the covers of the pulp, which carried a boast that it had been 'Selected by The Crime Jury,' were by Joe Farer.

Clues, Clayton's contribution to the new genre, appeared in 1926 and was launched by a varied group of authors including H. Bedford Jones, William Morrison Rouse, and Lemuel DeBra, who maintained he had been in the Secret Service for 13 years. It also ran

special features on true crime, including Herbert Mills's 'The Red Trail of Dope,' Detective McBride's accounts of actual cases in 'Detect-O-Grams,' and 'The Puzzle Chest,' in which readers' knowledge of criminology was tested by Helen Asbury. The imaginative and action-packed covers were the work of 'Wesso,' a Polish-born artist Hans Waldemar Wessolowksi, who had emigrated to the U.S. and found a ready market with the pulps. His reputation and enduring fame is, though, particularly based on the series of 34 covers that he produced for the Clayton company's science fiction magazine, *Astounding*.

After the collapse of the Clayton empire, *Clues* was taken over by Street & Smith, which appointed Anthony Rud as editor, and he encouraged a number of tougher writers such as Cleve F. Adams, James P. Hughes, and T. T. Flynn to fill the magazine's pages. Erle Stanley Gardner also made regular appearances, with a series about a brash young lawyer named Barney Killigen, who was not a million miles removed from the great Perry Mason. *Clues* finally closed in 1943.

It was back in 1920, however, that crime fiction saw the arrival of the single most important magazine in the genre, *Black Mask*. The origins of this legendary publication could not have been more unlikely. It was created by H. L. Mencken and George Jean Nathan, the owners of *The Smart Set* and *Saucy Stories*, simply because they were running short of money. In the summer of 1919, Mencken told his partner that their only hope of staying in business – and sustaining their own high-living lifestyles – was to 'get into the new cheap magazine scheme.'

He had noticed the success of *Detective Story Magazine* and decided that crime fiction was what the public were prepared to pay for. He suggested they utilize the figure of Satan wearing a mask, which appeared on the front cover of every issue of *The Smart Set*, as the name for their magazine – hence *Black Mask*.

Mencken asked Florence Osborne, one of the co-editors of *The Smart Set*, to edit the magazine, and told her she should re-use any crime-orientated stories that had been submitted to the society magazine. There was no point in chasing material until they had established whether or not the new pulp would succeed. He also suggested to his employee that she should print her name as F. M. Osborne on the title page

to give the impression a man was the editor – although it seems likely the magazine was making a gentle pitch for female readers with its subtitle (later dropped) 'A Magazine of Mystery, Romance, and Adventure.' However, the cover of the first issue for October 1920 gave a different impression. It showed a young girl cowering from a branding iron, which had left a smoking image on her cheek. The names of the contributors to the early issues of *Black Mask*, such as Bentley B. Mackay, W. Wheeler, and Bob Du Soe, mean little today, but the magazine caught on with readers, and by April 1919 it was selling over 200,000 copies per issue. Despite this success, Mencken's tone when referring to the pulp was always disparaging. He wrote to a friend that summer, denying the very formula that Smith had predicted would work:

'The *Black Mask* is a lousy magazine – all detective stories ... but it seems to be a success. I hear that Woodrow [Wilson, the president of the United States] reads it. Reading mss. for it is a fearful job, but it has kept us alive during a very bad year.'

Despite the continued rise in sales figures, nothing could persuade Mencken that the 'louse,' as he called *Black Mask*, was worth the trouble that

publishing it entailed ... 'The thing has burdened both Nathan and me with disagreeable work,' he complained in another letter that same year. So when the two partners received an offer for *Black Mask* from the Pro-Distribution Company on Madison Avenue, they did not hesitate. They were happy to accept a deal for $100,000 – not a bad return on an investment of less than $500, the two men must have thought: but it was peanuts compared to the fortune the magazine would make in the next 25 years.

The new owners saw only opportunities where Mencken and Nathan had seen problems, and under the editorship of Joseph T. Shaw, a former Army captain, *Black Mask* pioneered a new literary genre, the 'hardboiled detective story,' whose influence is still strong today. The magazine developed the talents of some of the greatest names in U.S. detective fiction, including Dashiell Hammett (*Black Mask* first published his classic stories, 'The Maltese Falcon,' 'Red Harvest,' and 'The Glass Key' in serial form), Raymond Chandler (his early short stories formed the basis of 'The Big Sleep' and 'Farewell, My Lovely'), Erle Stanley Gardner, George Harmon Coxe, Frank Gruber, and Carroll John Daly (who created the very first tough private eye, Race Williams, in the issue

It was in 1920 that crime fiction saw the arrival of the single most important magazine in the genre, *Black Mask.*

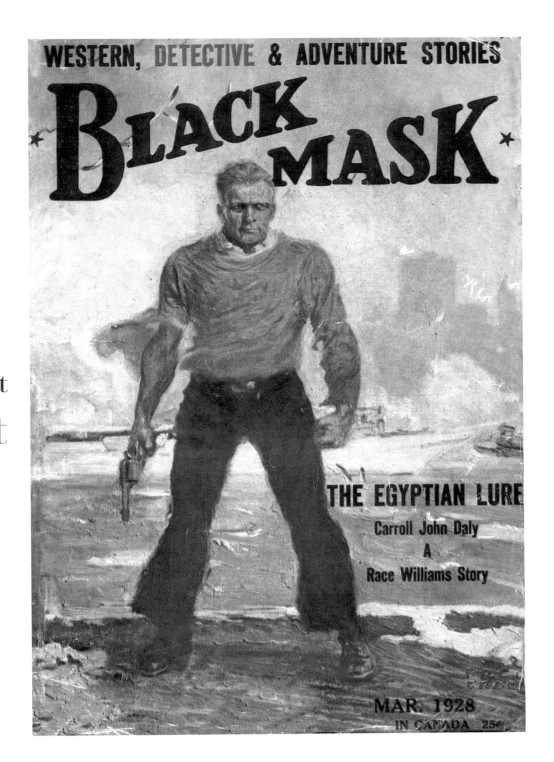

WESTERN, DETECTIVE & ADVENTURE STORIES

BLACK MASK

THE EGYPTIAN LURE

Carroll John Daly

A

Race Williams Story

MAR. 1928
IN CANADA 25¢

ABOVE

The original 'hardboiled dick,'
Race Williams, is pictured here
for Black Mask *by Fred Craft.*
(March, 1928)

of June 1923). Such a literary 'hero' could probably only have appeared at this time, in the decade of Prohibition and Depression, as Ron Goulart has explained in his excellent history of the crime pulps, *Cheap Thrills* (1972):

'There had always been aggressive, straight-shooting fiction heroes,' he wrote. 'But it took the mood of the 20s to add cynicism, detachment, a kind of guarded romanticism, and a compulsion toward action. The disillusionment that followed the War and the frustration over the mushrooming gangster control of the cities affected the detective story as much as it did mainstream fiction. The same things began to unsettle the private detectives that bothered the heroes of Hemingway, Dos Passos, and Fitzgerald.'

The first of this tough, cynical, and pragmatic breed of 'private dicks,' who operated in what *Black Mask* called 'a new Wild West' (i.e. the big cities of New York, Chicago, Miami, and Los Angeles) was Race Williams, created by Carroll John Daly, a New York film projectionist who, as a result, became the most popular writer in *Black Mask*. Williams, the prototype of a whole army of sleuths, had evolved from an earlier creation of Daly's, Three-Gun Mack, but proved such a success in cases like 'Knights of the Open Palm,' 'The Third Murderer,' and 'The Egyptian Lure' that the mere mention of his name on the magazine's cover could push sales up by 15 percent. When Williams was portrayed on the covers by Fred Craft, looking mean and aggressive with a gun in one of his clenched fists, sales would rise by another 5 percent. Inside *Black Mask*, Williams never failed to deliver the goods in a stream of tough, first-person vernacular that would soon be imitated by every writer trying to break into the hardboiled pulps:

'I closed my finger on the trigger and shot the gunman smack through the side of the head. Hard? Cold-blooded? Little respect for life? Maybe. But after all, it didn't seem to me to be the time to argue the point with the would-be killer.'

All the interior artwork of *Black Mask* was done by Arthur Rodman Bowker, who had a rather eccentric style that somehow just failed to capture the fast-paced, bullet-riddled, fist-flying action of the stories by Daly, Hammett, Chandler, and their contemporaries. With its continuing success in the 30s, the magazine also regularly employed two other cover artists. Their work is now among the most collected in the crime field: the grim and racy style of Rudolph Belarski, and Rafael De Soto's

ABOVE LEFT
The curious style of Arthur Rodman Bowker illustrated many of the stories in Black Mask, *such as 'Double For Danger' by Sinclair Gluck. (August, 1929)*

wonderful visualizations of menacing gangsters terrorizing helpless, pretty young women.

For most of the 1920s, *Black Mask* plowed its hardboiled furrow unchallenged, while *Detective Story Magazine*, *Detective Fiction Weekly*, and *Clues* stuck to more traditional crime-busting. The public appetite for both styles clearly existed because all four pulps thrived, each introducing new writers year upon year, including now familiar names like Cornell Woolrich, John D. MacDonald, and W. T. Ballard.

Indeed, it was not until 1932 that another publishing group, Popular Publications Inc., of 205 East 42nd Street in New York, broke into the crime genre with a cut-price competitor it called *Dime Detective*. Popular had been formed by Henry Steeger and Harold Goldsmith. They sensed the opportunities in pulp publishing in 1931, and launched *Western Rangers*, *Gang World*, and *Battle Aces*, selling them all at 5 and 10 cents below the opposition. They commissioned eye-catching covers for *Dime Detective* and bought in writers who had already made their names in the genre, including Carroll John Daly, Frederick C. Davis, Norvell W. Page, Roger Torrey, and even Raymond Chandler – who, in fact, wrote his last stories for the Popular magazine before graduating

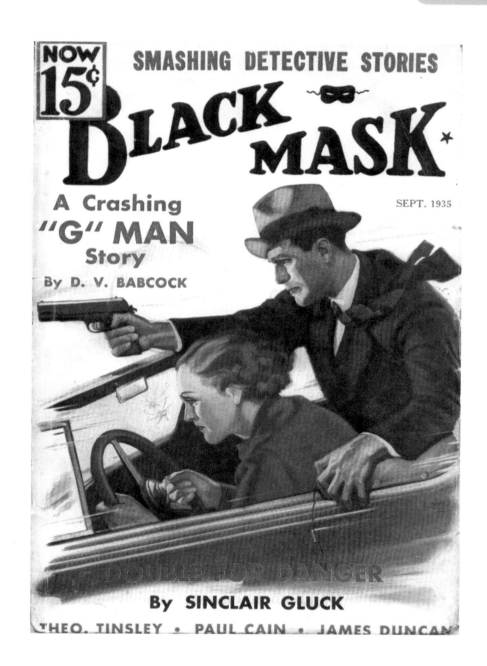

ABOVE

One of the great pulp artists, Rudolph Belarski regularly illustrated the cover of Black Mask. *(September, 1935)*

into hardcovers. Another key to the success of Popular Publications – which was replicated in several other genres as we shall see later in this book – was contained in a policy statement published in an early issue of *Dime Detective*:

'How many times have you paid good money for a magazine and gone home expecting many solid hours of good reading pleasure? How often have you found that you've picked a dud? Instead of the stimulating enjoyment of good fiction, you've found, neatly wrapped between two beguiling covers, a large order of sleep-producing nonsense! Popular Publications likes good covers. But more important than good covers are good stories – and Popular, with the largest total circulation of any fiction group, guarantees good stories!'

The editor of *Dime Detective* charged with fulfilling this claim was Kenneth Sheldon White, a man with a unique pedigree – his father, Trumbell White, had been the first editor of *Adventure*. The younger White made no bones

'Instead of good fiction, you've found, neatly wrapped between two beguiling covers, a large order of sleep-producing nonsense!'

about his admiration – envy even – for *Black Mask*, and had no compunction in luring away its writers with offers of better pay. He was also happy to publish offbeat stories by authors such as Norbert Davis, with his comic detective yarns, and Cornell Woolrich, with his grim fables of loneliness and murder. The prolific Erle Stanley Gardner was another of White's regular contributors, and it was Gardner's story 'Crimson Jade' in the September 1935 issue that inspired a notorious cover by the brilliant Walter Baumhofer – perhaps better known today for his artwork on the *Doc Savage* magazines. Captioned 'He Dangled Directly Over the Brazier,' it showed a private eye facing a far more horrible fate than the usual bullet or beating with a blunt instrument. Gardner's description was every bit as unsparing:

'Yow Sum Gay made a gesture to the two men. They picked Buckner up bodily, each one taking an end to the pole. A third man shoved a charcoal brazier toward the center of the room. Buckner noticed two ropes suspended from the ceiling. Each rope terminated in a loop. Two of the men each grasped a loop, placed it over an end of the bamboo pole, leaving Buckner dangling like the weight of some huge pendulum. The third man centered the brazier of charcoal directly under him. One of the men gave a push on the pole. Buckner started swinging back and forth. His body twisted and turned on the spit. The men pushed him, increasing the arc of his swing, until he was covering almost the entire width of the high-ceilinged room. At the lowest portion of each swing he cleared the brazier of glowing charcoal by not more than two inches.*

OPPOSITE

The tough, uncompromising style of Rafael De Soto made him a favorite with readers of Black Mask. *(November, 1942)*

ABOVE

A shock cover by Walter Baumhofer for perhaps the hardest of the hardboiled magazines, Dime Detective. *(September, 1935)*

'Buckner knew what was to happen. Slowly, inevitably, as remorseless as the incoming surge of an ocean tide, he would gradually swing through shorter arcs, until finally he would come to rest directly over the glowing charcoal ...'

There was no chance of a 'with one bound he was free' escape for the hapless Buckner. Like every other private dick in *Dime Detective* – and elsewhere for that matter – he had to suffer for his cause.

Most of the pulp's interior artwork was handled by John Fleming Gould, who revealed a keen eye for bizarre moments in the stories. Kenneth White also conducted a monthly column, 'Silk Dope,' in which he discussed the stories and, rare for its time, promoted his authors with detailed biographies, and occasionally photographs, although these were usually difficult to recognize when printed on pulp paper.

By a curious twist of fate, Popular Publications took over *Black Mask* in the early 40s, and Kenneth White, who had striven so hard to copy its formula, was handed the job of editing the magazine. Although he managed to secure the services of a number of the original contributors – and added several from the *Dime Detective* stable – sales declined as the decade passed, and he was forced to adopt a policy of publishing reprints. The great pioneer finally succumbed to market forces in 1953, and *Black Mask* was absorbed into the digest-sized *Ellery Queen's Mystery Magazine*.

Much earlier, in 1935, the popularity of *Dime Detective* had encouraged Steeger and Goldsmith to launch a companion pulp, *Detective Tales*. The aim this time was to offer 12 tough, action-packed stories for 10 cents. The writers were a mixture of veterans, such as Daly and Davis, and up-and-coming talents, of which there were several, including Richard Sale, who would later become a Hollywood scriptwriter and best-selling novelist. As a sales ploy, the magazine boasted that it included, among the dozen stories, a 'smashing, full-length novel,' which in actual fact took up no more than 20 of the pulp's 112 pages! The fiction was always ingeniously titled: 'There's Money in Corpses' and 'The Man Who Murdered Himself' being typical of many more. For some added value, *Detective Tales* ran two true-life features, 'Oddities of Crime' and 'The Crime Clinic.'

As the statement by Steeger and Goldsmith had maintained earlier, the pulp's covers and inside artwork were exemplary – in particular, the covers by Tom Lovell, whose gun-toting detectives, masked villains, and

OPPOSITE

Tom Lovell mixed menace and heroism in his covers for Detective Tales. *(September, 1936)*

OPPOSITE RIGHT

Giving a helping hand takes on a new meaning in this Tom Lovell illustration for Detective Tales. *(July, 1937)*

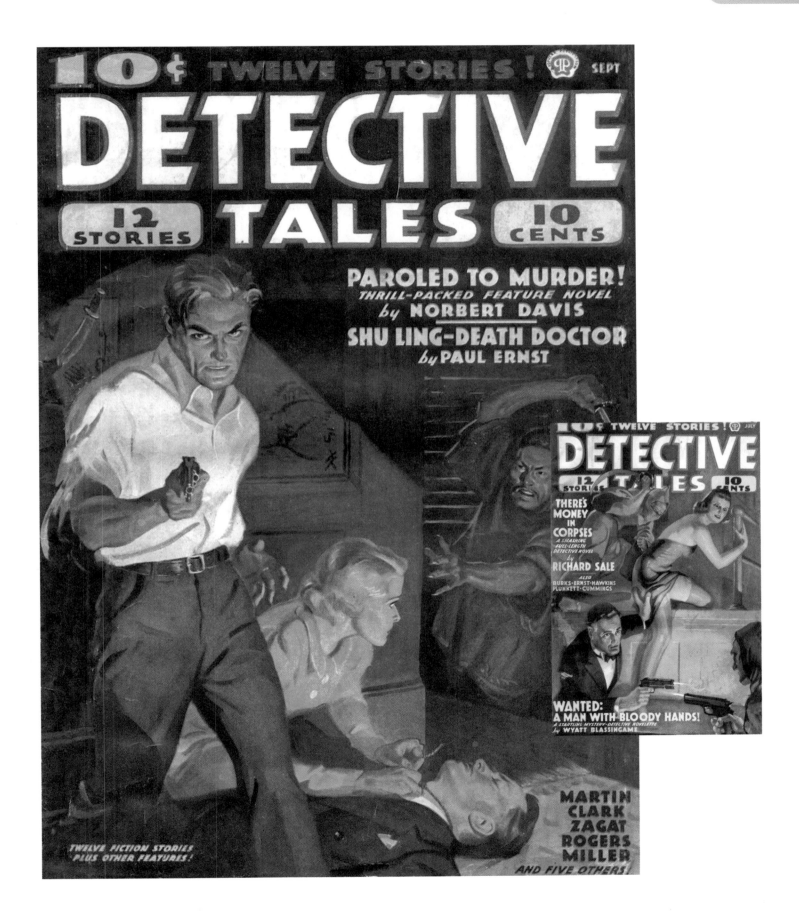

skulking Orientals were always distinctive. The interior artwork was created by a team including Will Ely, Peter Costanza, Fred Guardineer, Hamilton Green, Ralph Carlson, Paul Orban, and Amos Sewell. Both Green and Sewell were adept at handling the 'girl in a tricky situation,' which also became a staple ingredient of the spicy magazines and shudder pulps. *Detective Tales* continued to thrive until 1953, ultimately earning this rare tribute from historian Robert Sampson:

'It was a colorful, urgent, vigorous periodical, foaming with cheerful excesses; it was one of the classic pulp magazines.'

ABOVE LEFT

Hamilton Green illustrated many stories for Detective Tales *with touches of ingenuity, as shown in 'The Tick of Terror' by Ray Cummings. (July, 1938)*

A third Popular Publications magazine, *Ace G-Man Stories*, made its debut in 1936, focusing on stories about the special agents of the Federal Bureau of Investigation and Treasury Department in their war against organized crime. The main contributors were Paul Ernst (with tales like 'Death's Special Agent'), Wilson Cobb ('Last Laugh For Uncle Sam'), and the prodigious Norvell W. Page ('The Cop and the G-Man'). Malvin Singer, who had once wanted to be a police officer, provided the all-action covers of lone agents battling with massed ranks of mobsters, while Hamilton Greene and Monroe Eisenberg portrayed the equally heroic G-Men inside the magazine. An early issue of the pulp carried a 'Message from a G-Man,' in which the editor plugged the force with almost messianic fervor:

ABOVE RIGHT

Another fine example of Amos Sewell's talent, in this case for 'Corpse Without a Coffin' by Wayne Rogers for Detective Tales. *(September, 1936)*

'Everybody knows that sooner or later the most wary, the most desperate federal offender will be tracked to his lair – regardless of the complexity of detail required, or the time or the expense. No organization ever deserved more justifiably the wholehearted confidence which Americans invest in Mr. Hoover's super crime-fighting machine. Most people know (and if they don't, they should) that the F.B.I. recovers each year stolen property of many times more value than the operation costs of the entire department. They know of the decline of kidnappings; the exposition of crooked banking practises; and countless other services which are gradually helping to rid this country of the lawless.'

Unhappily such optimism – or perhaps the readers' failure to accept such lavish praise in the light of what was actually happening in the real world – condemned *Ace G-Man Stories* to a comparatively short existence. There were, however, to be two further crime pulps from Popular – *Strange Detective Mysteries* and *New Detective Magazine*. These fared rather better and lasted well into the 40s. *Strange Detective*, as the title implies, mixed bizarre crime with murder mysteries, and among the authors of forgettable

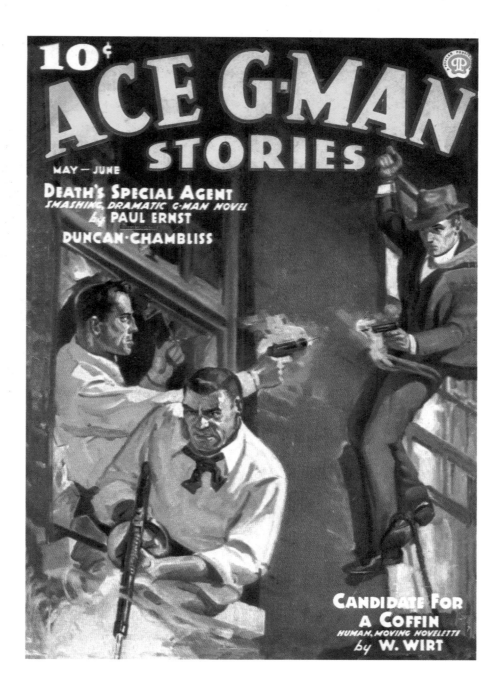

RIGHT

Malvin Singer was another expert at portraying scenes of violence, as he demonstrates here on the cover of Ace G-Man Stories. *(May/June, 1937)*

yarns like 'The Mansion of Missing Men,' 'The Talisman of Murder,' and 'Pardon My Ghoulish Laughter' could be found names more commonly associated with the mystery story genre, including Fredric Brown and G. T. Fleming-Roberts. In fact, the editor had boasted in the first issue of the magazine:

'Here – and here alone – on the pages of this magazine, you will find completely different, breathtaking stories of weirdly vivid mystery. That's our promise – and your guarantee of continued reading enjoyment!'

Rafael De Soto, whose work had been enhancing the covers of *Black Mask* for some years, was in evidence on a number of issues of *Strange Detective Mysteries*, and he also provided artwork for *New Detective Fiction*, which boasted above the title that it contained, 'The Best In Crime Fiction.' Frederick C. Davis and Bruno Fischer were

ABOVE LEFT

A new angle on an old trick was illustrated by Rafael De Soto for Strange Detective Mysteries. *(February, 1942)*

ABOVE RIGHT

Rafael De Soto updated the beauty and the beast motif for the cover of New Detective Magazine. *(July, 1946)*

notable contributors to the pulp, as was the young David Goodis, who is now acknowledged as one of the great writers of hardboiled fiction. Among the magazine's special features were 'Strange Trails To Murder,' drawn by Paul Lee, and M. E. Ohaver's column 'Solving Secrets,' which had appeared in *Detective Fiction Weekly* and now had a fresh start in *New Detective*.

Ned L. Pines was another astute New Yorker who got into the business of pulp publishing in 1931, after a casual meeting with a magazine distributor who told him he was desperate for new merchandise. Pines set up Better Publications Inc. at 22 West 48th Street and started off with two titles *Thrilling Love Stories* and *Thrilling Detective*. In the decade that followed, he and his astute editorial director and lifetime

LEFT
A hallmark of Thrilling Detective *was the offbeat cover artwork, which was rarely signed. (July, 1936)*

'Here you will find completely different, breathtaking stories of weirdly vivid mystery.'

friend, Leo Margulies, produced a whole series of pulp fiction magazines, ranging from westerns and true-life confessions to crime and hardboiled detectives – all of which were prefixed by the word 'Thrilling.' It turned out to be a

marketing strategy that paid handsome dividends, as Margulies remarked some years later:

'Ned liked to claim that our line was "probably the fastest selling bunch of all

10¢ **BLACK BOOK DETECTIVE**

FALL ISSUE

MURDER AMONG THE DYING
A Complete Tony Quinn Mystery Novel
By G. WAYMAN JONES

PROTECTIVE ARMOR
An Exciting Story
By NORMAN A. DANIELS

A *New* BLACK BAT MYSTERY NOVEL EVERY ISSUE

A THRILLING

'Thrilling Detective certainly ran a lot of fast-action tales about hardnosed and hardboiled detectives.'

the pulps." *Thrilling Detective* certainly ran a lot of fast-action tales about hardnosed and hardboiled detectives which readers just grabbed off the newsstands as soon as they came out each month.'

The success of *Thrilling Detective* was aided by Margulies's recruitment of versatile wordsmiths, including Carroll John Daly, W. T. Ballard, Roger Torrey, Wyatt Blassingame, and Robert Leslie Bellem – another prolific writer whose series about private eye Nick Ransom, who tackled every kind of criminal from gangland bosses to bow-and-arrow-wielding villains, became a favorite with readers.

Two years later, Ned Pines announced *Popular Detective*, which claimed 'Every Story Brand New,' and showcased what it called 'Complete Crime Novels.' Notable among these were the cases of 'Diamondstone,' a Magician-Sleuth written by G. T. Fleming-Roberts; Eugene Thomas's stories of Vivian Legrand, 'The Woman From Hell,' who described herself as 'utterly merciless and devoid of the usual human emotions' when matching

her wits against the most dangerous criminals in the underworld; and Simon Templar, a.k.a. 'The Saint,' created by the English writer Leslie Charteris, who was then living and working in Hollywood. Jack Kofoed contributed a long series of 'Historical Crimes,' which tended to concentrate on beautiful women gone wrong, such as the Countess de la Motte in 'The Affair of the Necklace.' The cover art of *Popular Detective* by Gordon Grant was always far superior to the anonymous interior artwork.

Pines was smart enough to realize that youngsters were also reading crime stories, and introduced two more pulps that featured 'masked crusaders' obviously aimed primarily at the youth market. *Black Book Detective*, which appeared under the 'Thrilling' banner in 1933, featured Special District Attorney Tony Quinn, the 'Nemesis of Crime,' who could change into a batlike figure, complete with huge sable wings, and leap over walls or hurtle through the air from skyscraper windows in pursuit of wrongdoers. He had a trio of helpers – Butch, Silk, and the beautiful Carol. The stories by G. Wayman Jones

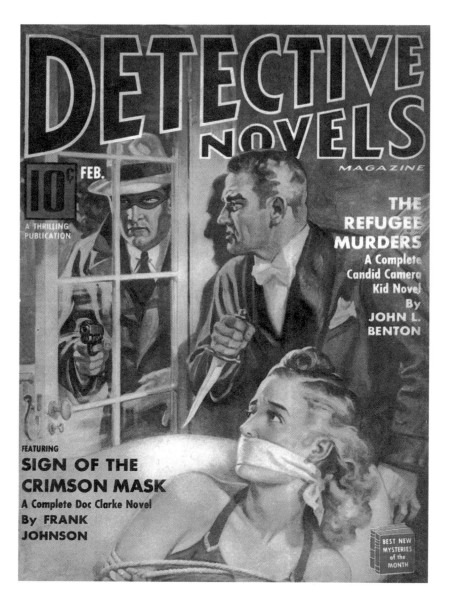

Doc Clarke was a pulp hero who wore only an eye mask as disguise. The artist who drew him for the covers of Detective Novels *did not sign his name. (February, 1941)*

Despite its title, 'Thrilling' *Detective Novels* was a short story magazine that just happened to carry two novelettes in every issue. The great favorite was the series about Dr. Robert Clarke, a medical practitioner who used his scientific knowledge and a ridiculous eye-mask to double as 'The Crimson Mask,' bringing to justice any number of criminals, from big-city fraudsters to small-time crooks. The stories were written in a rumbustious style by Frank Johnson. Another series character who scored well with the younger audience was Jerry Wade, known as 'The Candid Camera Kid,' who had an unerring ability to be on the spot and help in the arrest of criminals – thereby getting himself an exclusive front-page picture for his employers. John L. Benton wrote this long-running series. One reader was so enthusiastic about these two characters that he wrote to the editor in February 1941:

'The Candid Camera Kid and Doc Clarke are the two greatest characters in current crime fiction. They make a double feature of thrills exciting enough to satisfy any detective story fan!'

What editor could ask for more? The team of Ned Pines and Leo Margulies later founded a paperback line called Popular Library, which

were illustrated on the covers by Rudolph Belarski, with interior art by Ray Gamsey. The pulp also carried short stories by Norman A. Daniels, Joe Archibald, and Wayland Rice, with the occasional reprint of stories about other avengers, including England's 'Gentleman Cracksman' Raffles!

became famous for its crime and mystery list, containing titles by many of the authors that Pines and Margulies had used in the pulps, including Leslie Charteris, Craig Rice, Rufus King, and Anthony Boucher.

Aaron A. Wyn was perhaps the most unlikely figure to have become a pulp magnate, via the series of 'Ace' titles that he issued under the banner of Periodical House from 67 West 44th Street in New York. Born in Wyoming, he had begun his working life as a cowboy, followed by stints as a merchant seaman and schoolteacher, before ending up in New York editing manuscripts for Dell Publishing. In partnership with his wife, Rose, he decided to set up Periodical House and get into the pulp market. Aided by a widely experienced managing editor, Harry Widmer, the firm issued *Ten Detective Aces* in 1933, carrying an 'Ace of Spades' symbol to distinguish the line from the others, along with a slogan, '10 Stories for 10 Cents.' Widmer bought material from many tried and tested detective writers, including Lester Dent, W. T. Ballard, and Joe Archibald, always adhering to his boss's maxim:

'The story's the thing – good writing never has spoiled a well-plotted pulp story, but it never made a bad one good.'

Wyn is also remembered with admiration by his writers and fellow publishers for responding to any attacks that were made on the pulps in the media. When the *New York Times*, for example, castigated the magazines for being 'a little known and certainly officially unrecognized business in which the volume of production is more important than literary quality,' Wyn at once fired off a reply:

'Far from being unrecognized,' he declared, 'it [the pulp magazine industry] caters to 30 million readers a month and pays writers more than $1,500,000 per year.'

Norman Saunders, an artist whose work would become familiar in the horror pulps, provided many of the covers for *Ten Detective Aces*. He liked to show girls holding their own in dangerous situations – a tendency he would have to reverse for his other clients. The illustrations inside were mainly by Joe Chambers. The magazine contained a large proportion of advertisements offering readers the chance to train as 'Secret Service Operators,' purchase six shot pistols that fired tear gas 'to instantly stop, stun, and incapacitate the most vicious man,' and even buy shoulder holsters to carry the weapons for just $1.75.

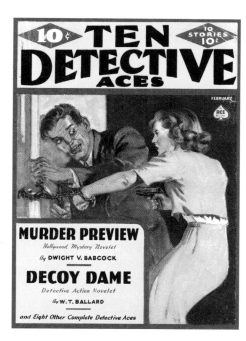

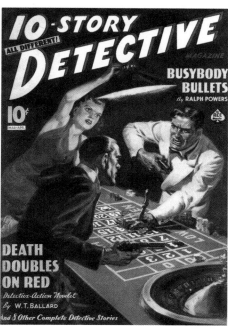

GANGSTER STORIES

25¢

MARCH

The Crime Crusade

Another Complete Serrano Novel by Anatole Feldman

AN ILLUSTRATED MAGAZINE

The magazine carried a high proportion of advertisements offering readers the chance to train as 'Secret Service Operators.'

The success of *Ten Detective Aces* was the foundation on which A. A. Wyn built his pulp empire, which consisted of a string of western, adventure, sport, aviation, and love pulps, plus three more crime titles – *10-Story Detective*, *Variety Detective*, and *Secret Agent X*, which featured another crime fighter leading a double life, written by Paul Chadwick. Of this trio, *10-Story Detective* probably enjoyed the greatest success and certainly had the higher literary content, running hardboiled stories by W. T. Ballard, Eric Lennox, and Cliff Howe. Again, Saunders and Chambers were the major illustrators.

Amongst all these crime and hardboiled pulps, the occasional novelty title appeared, offering a different slant on the genre – *Gangster Stories*, *True Gang Life*, and *The Underworld Magazine* were typical of their kind. The magazines had a tendency to glorify mobsters and hoods, and although some readers may have enjoyed the particularly hardboiled writing found between their covers, the authorities unfortunately did not. Regularly seized from bookstalls, and condemned by civic groups, these pulps did not last very long.

Gangster Stories, described as 'An Illustrated Magazine of Racketeers and Gun Molls,' was issued by the Blue Band Publishing Corporation at 570 Seventh Avenue. Among its most popular features was an 'anonymous' series called 'Ex-Gun Moll.' The stories were about Big Nose Serrano, the singing Assemblyman, and his 'Crime Crusade' in the 'Bloody Tenth' [District], written by Anatole Feldman, and the experiences of Fay Laurence, a beautiful if rather naive 'sob sister' (newspaper reporter), who specialized in interviewing big shot gangsters in yarns with extraordinary titles like 'One Second of Sex,' written by C. B. Yorke. The covers and stories in *Gangster Stories* were illustrated by the versatile Tom Lovell. The pulp also had a monthly offer worth $10 to readers who sent in 'The Best Newspaper Clipping of Gangster News,' and a couple of pages of editor's chat entitled 'The Eavesdropper.' This was written in gangster vernacular and readers were referred to as 'roddies.'

Notwithstanding its title, *True Gang Life*, published by Associated Authors Inc. of 11 West 42nd Street, New York, consisted almost entirely of fiction produced by a circle of authors including Steve Fisher, Gilbert Langen, Ralph Milne Farley, and Raymond A. Palmer – the last two of whom became better known as stalwarts of the science fiction genre. Story titles like 'Mop-Up Mary' by Charles B. McCray, 'Hoppy Calls The Tune' by Donald

ABOVE

An anonymous illustration for the 'Ex-Gun Moll' series in Gangster Stories. *(April, 1932)*

OPPOSITE

The archetypal mobster, as envisaged by Tom Lovell for Gangster Stories. *(March, 1932)*

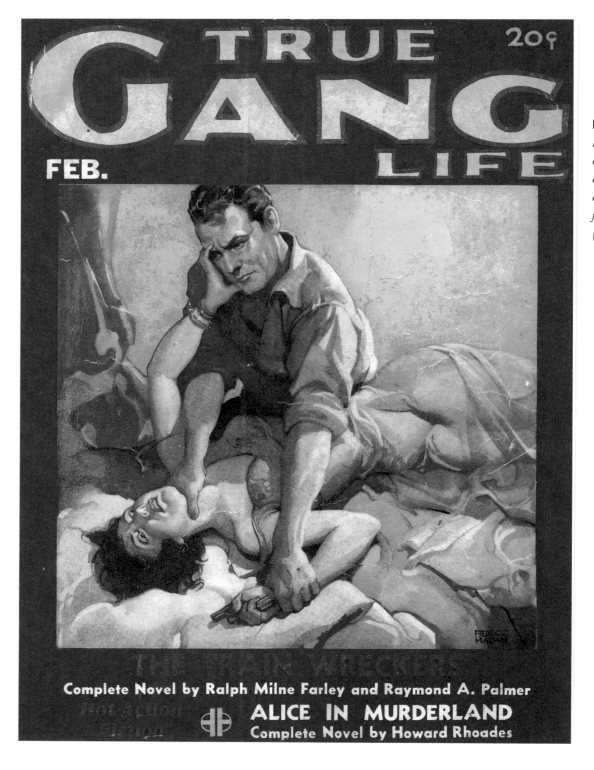

LEFT
Fredric Madan
created a series of
covers that mixed
color and brutality
for Fredric Madan *True Gang Life.*
(February, 1935)

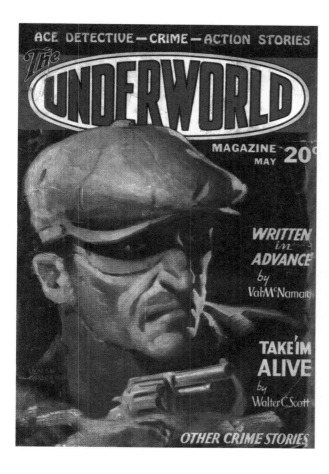

S. Aitken, and the dreadfully punning 'Alice in Murderland' by Howard R. Rhoades give a pretty clear idea of the contents. The poor-quality illustrations inside, by an artist who signed himself 'TDS,' were offset by Fredric C. Madan's wonderfully garish, if brutal, covers.

The last of this trio of examples of novelty titles, *Underworld Magazine*, embraced the wider fields of crime, from crooked businessmen to organized crime, and must have surprised honest readers with 'Crime Specials' such as 'Safe-cracking – A Vanishing Art,' signed 'Incognito.' Published by the Carwood Publishing Company of Springfield, Massachusetts, which maintained editorial offices at 551 Fifth Avenue in New York, the contributors were less familiar names such as Val

McNamara, Walter C. Scott, and Charles J. Sullivan, all more than likely moonlighting writers from the major crime pulps using pseudonyms. A notable aspect of the magazine was the striking artwork, both on the covers and inside, by Lyman Anderson.

One further title will complete this section: *Private Detective*, a guns-blazing, girl-bashing, mobster-dominated pulp issued in 1937 by the Trojan Publishing Corporation of 125 East 46th Street, New York, bearing the slogan, 'Intimate Revelations of Private Investigators.' Legend has it that the company was named for the well-known American contraceptive of the same name, although such items seemed farthest from the thoughts of the violent men and ripe females whose activities were chronicled by such accomplished

hardboiled yarn spinners as Roger Torrey, Ken Cooper, and Robert Leslie Bellem. The truth was that Trojan was an associate company of Culture Publications, whose partners, Frank Armer and Harry Donenfield, had been responsible for the first line of spicy pulps. The influence was there for all to see in *Private Detective*, in stories with titles like 'Escort Service,' 'Queen of Diamonds,' and 'Connoisseur of Death,' not to mention the powerful cover artwork by William Parkhurst. Pages of advertisements for books on 'Sex Secrets' and 'Corporal Punishment,' 'Spicy Home Movies,' and photographs of 'Rare Paris Nudes' only underlined the impression that *Private Detective* represented a whole new dimension of reading experiences. A dimension that became known as the 'spicy pulps.'

ABOVE LEFT
This portrait of a cracksman by the talented Lyman Anderson was created for The Underworld Magazine. *(May, 1932)*

ABOVE RIGHT
H. V. Parkhurst combined violence and sexuality with great effect on his covers for Private Detective. *(April, 1935)*

★ AUG. 25¢

Spicy DETECTIVE STORIES

TWO HANDS TO CHOKE
by Colby Quinn

The Spice *of* Life and Lust

THE SPICY PULPS

The name Culture Publications Inc. was a tongue-in-cheek misnomer, typical of the opportunist world of the pulps – all the more so because the company became notorious for its stable of sex and violence magazines.

RIGHT
This helpless victim was featured on a cover for Spicy Mystery Stories. *(July, 1936)*
(See page 92)

OPPOSITE
The brutal and erotic covers by H. J. Ward became a hallmark of Spicy Detective *and the other titles in the series. (August, 1936)*

ulture Publications launched a series of spicy titles in 1933 that, for almost 10 years, raised the imaginations and libidos of American men almost to fever pitch. Certainly the hot pulps that had preceded them provided readers with a melange of inferred sex and pseudosophistication, but what the folks at Culture had in mind was another line of 'U.T.C.' magazines in which eroticism was taken a whole step further. The spicy decade – and in particular the four Culture titles that began it – *Spicy Detective Stories, Spicy Adventure Stories, Spicy Western Stories,* and *Spicy Mystery Stories* – left an indelible mark on pulp history. For in their pages, sexual desire was indulged in full for the first time.

The men who created the concept were Harry Donenfeld, a printer and distributor, and Frank Armer, a publisher. They set up business at 480 Lexington Avenue in Manhattan, their sights set on America's private parts. Culture Publications was only one of the corporate names that the two men used – Trojan Publishing, with its association with contraceptives, was another – and the accommodation address to which readers of all their magazines had to write was innocuous Market Street in far-away Wilmington, Delaware. Donenfeld's and Armer's idea was simple enough: to take the genres that were already popular with pulp magazine readers – detection, adventure, mystery, and the Wild West – and lace them with lust, lechery,

violence, and even a little sadism. Just the kind of 'hot stuff' – the pair reckoned – that would appeal to U.S. males smarting under the effects of the Depression.

The line was launched in April 1934, with *Spicy Detective*. Veteran pulp editor Lawrence Cadman was hired to edit the magazine and its companion pulps and, for guidance, he was given a letter that Frank Armer had written earlier to an author friend. A surviving copy indicates that the publisher had given considerable thought to his market and the restrictions that existed. It makes fascinating, not to say revealing, reading:

'On account of the attitude of certain groups of people in different parts of the

ABOVE

Jack Lokoli illustrated dramatic incidents with a minimum of line work and a maximum of effect, as shown in this illustration for 'Murder By The Book' by Cay Moran for Spicy Detective. *(October, 1936)*

country, it is necessary that we use great discretion in the amount of sex we have in the stories run in *Spicy Detective*. It is difficult to lay down hard and fast rules, as opinions differ greatly in this matter. However, there are a few things I wish to call to your attention which should be considered when you are writing stories for the magazine.

'If it is necessary for the story to have a girl give herself to a man, or be taken by him, do not go too carefully into the details. You can lead up to the actual consummation, but leave the actual act entirely up to the reader's imagination. This subject should be handled delicately and a great deal can be done by implication and suggestion.

'Whenever possible, avoid complete nudity of the female characters. You can have a girl strip down to her underwear, or transparent negligée or nightgown, or the thin, torn shreds of her garments, but while the girl is alive and in contact with a man, we do not want complete nudity. A nude female corpse is allowable, of course. Also, a girl undressing in the privacy of her own room, but when men are in the action, try to keep at least a shred of something on the girls. Do not have men in underwear in scenes with women, and no nude men at all.

'The idea is to have a very strong sex element in these stories without anything that might be interpreted as being vulgar or obscene. Sometimes it is difficult to draw the line exactly, but if you are not carried away too far by your enthusiasm of the moment, it can usually be handled properly.'

The evidence suggests that 'difficult' was exactly what it amounted to when trying to draw the line for *Spicy Detective*, although it is equally clear from reading the first year's issues that it was not long before both publisher and authors were getting carried away in their enthusiasm for making profit and selling stories. Right from the first number, the lush cover art by H. J. Ward more than hinted at forbidden fruits. Indeed, Ward was to become the star of the spicy titles with his pictures of attractive young girls, who might almost be the girl-next-door – although few would probably ever have to face the terrifying situations encountered by the spicy girls. Tony Goodstone has provided a vivid description of the landmark April 1934 issue:

'On its cover, cowering in the foreground, was a tender but terrified blonde, clad only in the flimsiest of undergarments, one limp stocking dangling around her ankle. At her feet were a few fragments of her dress. The rest of it was clutched in the apelike fist

'You can have a girl strip down to her underwear, or transparent negligée or nightgown, or the thin, torn shreds of her garments.'

His **reward** for saving the lovely creature was invariably the enjoyment of the luscious charms she had so valiantly denied her tormentors.

of the object of her terror – a man behind her, ready to spring. He was small and compact. A black vest half covered his shoulder-holster. A white shirt made him look even swarthier than he was. His black hair was wild, his teeth were bared in a suggestive leer. His face was bloody where it had been raked by the girl's fingernails. There was no mistaking his intention. The title of the cover-story was next to the girl's knee – 'The Love Nest Murder' by Jon Le Baron. There was no mistaking Culture Publications' intention, either.'

Lawrence Cadman did not take long to assemble a team of accomplished wordsmiths who knew how to fuel male fantasies. Although the names of these men mean very little today, it is safe to assume that quite a few were pseudonyms. Typical contributions to *Spicy Detective*, such as 'Dead Girls Don't Talk' by John Ryan, 'Pretty Corpse' by William Decatur, and '38 Calibre Kisses' by Peter Grant, were all raunchy tales featuring pretty young women threatened with being stripped, beaten, tortured, or even mutilated by any number of merciless gangsters or violent criminals. Yet in all of them lurked a hero who would arrive in the nick of time and overcome the most fearsome odds to rescue the girl. His reward for saving the lovely creature was invariably the enjoyment of the luscious charms she had so valiantly denied her tormentors. Sometimes there was the hint of rape in the stories as this extract from 'Too Many Clues' by John Wayne reveals:

'With that he hooked his fingers inside the neck of her dress and jerked. The silk parted and ripped halfway to her waist. Eyes wide with panic, Marcia tried to run. But Paietto caught her roughly from behind. Then she fought with him and sobbed, "Oh, God! Let me go!" Marcia was helpless with terror and scarcely realized what was being done to her.*

OPPOSITE

The tough private eye Dan Turner works over another suspect in this illustration by H. J. Ward for Spicy Detective. *(November, 1942)*

25¢ ★ NOV.

Spicy DETECTIVE

DARK ROOM
KEEP OUT

Buy
WAR BONDS AND STAMPS
FOR VICTORY

RIDDLE IN RED

by
Robert Leslie Bellem

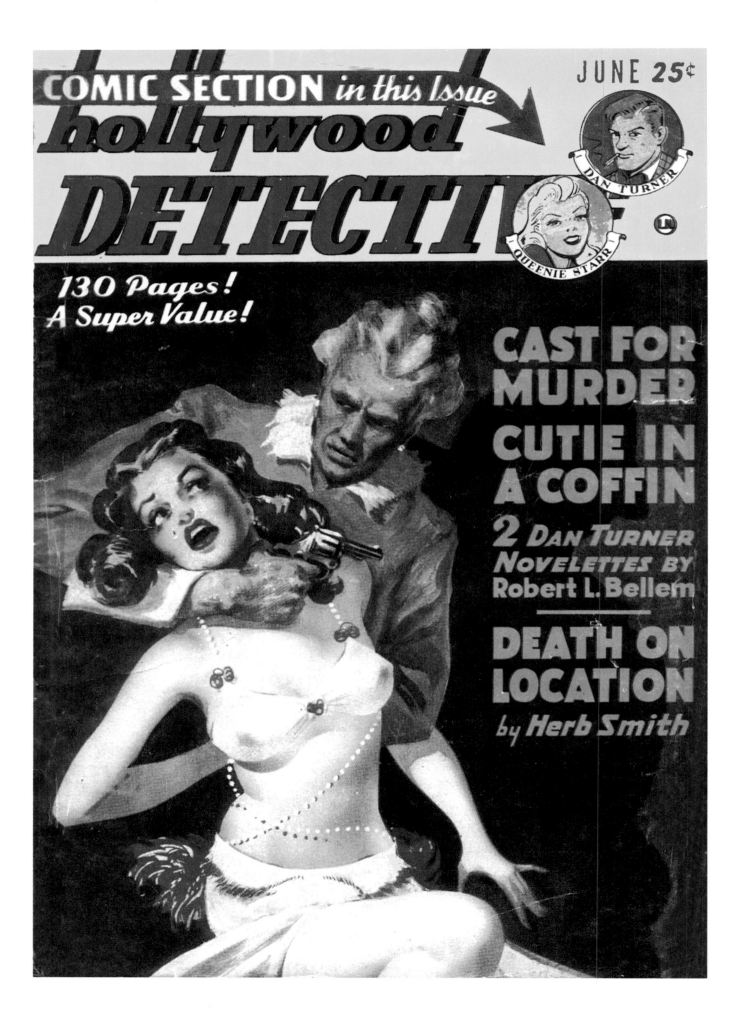

'Paietto ogled her trembling loveliness with ghoulish anticipation, stalking her while she fearfully retreated. Her arms were locked across the vulnerability of her breasts, but she was otherwise an undefended, exciting lure, a feast to the eye, under a slip that concealed virtually nothing. Paietto sprang with a headlong lunge and snared her around the waist, Marcia struggled hysterically. Her legs were suddenly whirled into the air and she was hurled flat onto the studio floor ...'

Occasionally, readers were treated to accounts of women fighting women, as in 'Murder By The Book' by Cay Moran:

'"Damn you, damn you!" screamed the blonde and leaped to her feet. In a split second she was across the room. She seized Lorraine McClain's shoulder, hurled her away so violently that the material of her silk gown tore to reveal swaying, scantily brassiered breasts, quickly smothered in protecting palms. "Are you accusing me of killing my own friend, Benny McClain?" she screamed

again. "I'll beat the truth out of you, damn you!"'

This particular story was illustrated by Jack Lokoli, who provided bold and provocative illustrations for many Spicy Detective stories.

Two months after its launch, Spicy Detective ran a story featuring a new kind of private detective, Dan Turner, who worked in Hollywood and specialized in movie mayhem. Turner, who proved as quick at using his fists and his gun (which he always referred to as a 'roscoe') as he was at getting into bed with women clients (and, sometimes, even female suspects), was the creation of Robert Leslie Bellem, a former LA newspaper reporter, whose prose style mixed hardboiled roughhouse with a Runyonesque sense of humor. Over the next few years, Bellem became the most prolific contributor to the Culture Publications titles and also one of the fastest pulp wordsmiths. It was Bellem who coined

the immortal phrase 'as human as the next gazabo' for the feelings experienced by any man who has just rescued a girl from a fate much worse than death. And who could fail to enjoy these lines from the Dan Turner caper, 'Riddle In Red:'

'Trixie wrapped herself around me, turned on the steam. Her voluptuous breasts flattened against my shirt front and the fragrance of her sunset hair drifted into my sniffer. Firecrackers went off in my capillaries and I felt my self-control slipping its moorings. After all, you can take just so much of that stuff;

OPPOSITE
Keats Petree provided the cover artwork for Dan Turner's own pulp, Hollywood Detective. *(June, 1950)*

ABOVE LEFT
This is a typically brutal moment from a Dan Turner caper in 'Dead Man's Head' by Robert Leslie Bellem for Spicy Detective Stories. *(October, 1941)*

ABOVE
The accident-prone Sally the Sleuth's cartoon strip series was drawn by Adolphe Barreaux for Spicy Detective Stories. *(May, 1938) (See page 88)*

'For the next few minutes, all I knew was that I had a cargo of lovely red-haired fire blazing in my embrace; and there was only one way to quench the flames.'

and then you go off the deep end. I forgot all about the knuckle-dusting Noonan had handed me that afternoon; lost track of my original purpose in coming here. For the next few minutes, all I knew was that I had a cargo of lovely red-haired fire blazing in my embrace; and there was only one way to quench the flames. After all, what the hell?'

It was to hell and back (or at least the murky streets of Hollywood) that Turner's cases took him in pursuit of willing female flesh – and not so willing at times, because Turner was not above hitting or smacking wayward girls – and a stream of crooked actors and actresses, murderous producers, sadistic directors, and some notable archvillains, including one who liked to decapitate his victims and send the heads to the private eye! Such was the popularity of the series that Donenfeld and Armer later gave Turner his own pulp, *Hollywood Detective*, under the Trojan banner. (As if to underline the sexual connection, the sleuth never drank anything but Vat 69.) This pulp ran into the 50s, with Robert Leslie Bellem writing the vast majority of the contents himself. It is perhaps no surprise to learn that after the pulps folded, Bellem switched to writing for films and television, and his credits include *The Lone Ranger*, *Tarzan*, *77 Sunset Strip*, and another of the classic hardmen, *Dick Tracy*.

The interior illustrations for the Turner stories were by Max Plaisted, who had worked for several years on newspapers before joining the Culture

ABOVE
Another pulp heroine prone to losing her clothes, Queenie Starr, was drawn by Keats Petree, whose strip adventures appeared in Spicy Detective Stories. *(July, 1950)*

OPPOSITE
Artist H. J. Ward was just as much at home illustrating the covers of Spicy Adventure Stories *as any of the other spicy titles he worked for. (June, 1940)*

Publications team of artists. The popularity of the private eye ensured Plaisted plenty of work in the pages of *Spicy Detective*, and later he drew a cartoon series featuring Turner for *Hollywood Detective*. *Spicy Detective*, in fact, ran one of the first picture strips in the pulps, certainly the first to star a woman, Sally The Sleuth, created by Adolphe Barreaux, who later became editor of *Hollywood Detective*. Sally was an inquisitive, well-endowed young undercover cop who invariably lost her clothes while tackling criminal maniacs for her handsome boss, known only as 'The Chief.' Later she was joined by 'Queenie Starr: Glamor Girl of Hollywood' (drawn by Keats Petree), a girl with an equal ability to shed her clothes in tight corners – although this seemed only to enhance her career as a film star.

When Culture Publications added a second title to their line, *Spicy Adventure Stories*, the prolific Robert Leslie Bellem's name was soon to be found among the list of contributors, coupled with a handful of other names familiar to readers of risqué fiction, such as Ken Cooper and Clayton Maxwell. The first issue boasted:

'Nowhere but in *Spicy Adventure Stories* can you find such yarns. All the thrilling action of old-style adventure yarns in the far-places of the earth. ADDED to that, the glamorous romance of beautiful girls, of daring love ...'

The titles of the stories were no doubt intended to intrigue readers still further: 'Blood in the Desert' by Saul W. Paul ('Buried alive! Was that to be his fate for daring the Sheikh and snatching a white girl from an oriental slave market?'), 'Temple of Eternity' by Cliff Ferris ('"I shall make you Emperor of the World," she told him, and, in spite of his love for Lea, he was tempted by what she showed him on top of the temple!'), and 'Lecher's Cargo' by Ken Cooper ('The captain was king of the slave ship, where torture and lust lurked below decks') – an epic which, from the first paragraph, catapulted readers into a world of sado-eroticism:

'The hairy hand of Jenson Werner, captain of the Melbourne Prince, *a derelict tramp sailing the waters of the Pacific, slid over the naked shoulder of the girl, his stubbed, coarse fingers reaching for the lush warmness of her ecru breasts. She drew away as he reached his*

ABOVE

Exotic locations and violence against helpless women were a staple ingredient in Spicy Adventure Stories. *This is an illustration by Bert Low for 'Blood in the Desert' by Tom Kane. (February, 1939)*

'All the thrilling action of old-style adventure yarns in the far-places of the earth. Added to that, the glamorous romance of beautiful girls, of daring love ...'

ABOVE

Diana Daw and her clothes regularly parted company in the series drawn by Clayton Maxwell for Spicy Adventure Stories. *(June, 1935)*

ABOVE LEFT

This highly evocative
H. J. Ward cover was drawn
for Spicy Western Stories.
(December, 1936)

ABOVE

Cowboys invariably handled their women
badly in Spicy Western Stories, allowing
H. J. Ward full rein for his talent.
(January, 1937)

'His eyes fiery, tongue hanging from slobbering lips, Remark leaned, grabbed her, spilled her to the floor.'

goal, but not before his cupped hands had caught in the bodice of her cotton dress and torn it away. Werner licked his gross lips. It had been a long time since Santa Cruz had produced such a one as this ...'

H. J. Ward was again the most regular cover artist for *Spicy Adventure Stories*, with Max Plaisted providing a lot of the interior artwork in conjunction with Bert Low, whose powerfully erotic illustrations revealed a talent for depicting sexuality, violence, and bondage in exotic locations. Clayton Maxwell drew the strip cartoon adventures of Diana Daw, another *femme* who was more often without her clothes than in them during her adventures all over the world.

The settings were far less exotic and life was much grittier in the American West, as was portrayed in *Spicy Western Stories* – although the girls were just as gorgeous, vulnerable, and likely to be caught in their underwear. The bad guys, too, were just as driven by lust and cruelty as their compatriots in the other spicy mags. This had much to do with the fact that the same authors were busy writing the stories – 'Gunsmoke Passion' by 'Justin Case', for example, was Robert Leslie Bellem yet again – while versatile authors from the other pulps, including E. Hoffman Price, contributed frequent tales of flaring guns and tearing calico, such as 'Treason's Kiss' and 'Killer's Girl.' The magazine also had its undressed comic-strip heroine, Polly of the Plains, plus

the artwork of two line artists, Harry Smilkstein and H. V. Parkhurst, with a flair for bedroom scenes, where the West really got wild. In *Spicy Western Stories* it was certainly more than just gunbelts that got unbuckled and cattle that were roped, as this extract from Paul Richard's 'Gravy Train' demonstrates:

'Jup Remark gulped with a horsey sound, growled, went after Nancy. His eyes fiery, tongue hanging from slobbering lips, Remark leaned, grabbed her, spilled her to the floor. He grabbed her slender ankles and laughed at his own brute strength as he lifted her level with his shoulders, her head swinging clear of the floor. Helpless, she pounded at his legs with futile little fists. He circled her knees with one arm, and

ABOVE RIGHT
Sex and violence were regular occurrences in the West, according to this illustration by H. V. Parkhurst for 'Trigger Law' by Wilbur Brown, featured in Spicy Western Stories. *(March, 1938)*

ABOVE LEFT

The hand of fate strikes again at a helpless young beauty in Morgan Lafay's story, 'Her Demon Lover,' illustrated by H. J. Ward for Spicy Mystery Stories. (July, 1936)

ABOVE

New title, same ingredients – H. J. Ward once again produced the cover art for Spicy Mystery Stories.
(July, 1935)

her skirt fell downward, over her head, forming a sack. Her white legs, bare above the stockings, thrashed desperately, impotently within his powerful grasp. Her voice, small, frantic, muffled, came through the skirt ...'

The authors working for Culture Publications gave free rein to their imaginations when writing for the last of the company's quartet of pulps, *Spicy Mystery Stories*. Robert Leslie Bellem – as ever – chipped in grisly tales like 'Fiend's Feast' and 'Death's Nocturne,' E. Hoffman Price recounted the horrors of the 'Tailor Made Dummy' and 'The Garden of Evil.' For gory good measure, readers could read about the 'Devil Doctor' by Lew Merrill, wander into Arthur Wallace's 'Dungeons for the Blind,' and enter – if they dared – Saul W. Paul's 'Temple of Terror,' which featured the kind of mad cultist and female victims that regularly appeared in this kind of overheated fiction:

'Footsteps slapped the stone and drew Lane's gaze away from the fire. Toward the other end of the big subterranean chamber, evidently a cellar beneath the temple, a group of Creed's votaries huddled. Some were garbed in loose, brown robes. Others were nude, except for a loin cloth or girdle, bearing the bloody prints of the lash on back and bosom. The leaping flames provided the only illumination, painting the eerie scene with hellish red light. The faces of the devotees were diabolical, twisted with an evil blood lust. From the heavy shadow beyond the rim of firelight, two brown-robed figures emerged bearing a limp burden. Icy talons gripped Lane's heart, and a groan wrenched from his lips, as he recognized the form of Lila Drew, bound hand and foot like himself. The robed ones deposited the girl beside Lane, retreated to join their brethren. They all commenced a weird, toneless chant:

"Ye have sinned and not repented – Satan comes to claim his own!"'

Occasionally, the fiends in *Spicy Mystery Stories* came in the most beautiful forms – only to reveal their real nature once they had some hapless male victim worked up into a lather of anticipation. Arthur Humbolt describes just such a *femme fatale* in 'Hands of the Dead:'

'Her perfect body was in its most perfect setting, a pale pink negligée that made her dark loveliness infinitely more desirable than stark nudity. Carelessly, the sheer fabric about the firm, pouting

ABOVE LEFT
This typical situation from a Robert Leslie Bellem story, 'Death's Nocturne,' appeared in Spicy Mystery Stories.
(July, 1937)

'Her perfect body was in its most perfect setting, a pale pink negligée that made her dark loveliness infinitely more desirable than stark nudity.'

mounds of her breasts quivered ravishingly with her rapid breathing. Then, hugging the warm contours of her plump torso, the revealing cloth molded the eye-pleasing curves of her hips, spread an easily penetrable veil before milky thighs and legs that were veritable poems of girl-flesh. Her lips, passionate curves of bee-stung crimson, parted as she leaned toward Hugh, revealing at that moment a row of white, sharp-pointed teeth ...'

Spicy Mystery Stories had its own comic-strip heroine in Olga Mesmer, a beguiling creature who fought on the side of good against a series of villains with supernatural powers. ('The Astounding Adventures of Olga Mesmer,' drawn by Bob Stone, took her from the farthest regions of the earth to the planet Venus.) H. J. Ward's screaming beauties in the grasp of every kind of fiend were a major attraction for readers of *Spicy Mystery Stories*. Inside the magazine, H. V. Parkhurst was partnered by an artist, with a skill for drawing the naked female form, who

has left no more trace of his identity than the initial 'N.' He also pictured degenerates of all kinds mauling one luckless female after another.

Apart from their readers, the spicy magazines had fans in unexpected places – but nowhere more surprising than in the columns of the *New Yorker*, the monitor of society, fashion, and the arts. In 1941, one of the periodical's leading writers, S. J. Perelman, devoted a column to the magazines and Dan Turner in particular. The piece was called, 'Somewhere a Roscoe ...' and in it Perelman declared:

'Call it a schoolboy crush, puppy love, the senseless infatuation of a callow youth for a middle-aged, worldly wise publishing house, but I love Culture Publications not only for *Spicy Detective*, but also *Spicy Mystery*, *Spicy Adventure*, and *Spicy Western*.'

He went on in a mixture of affection and gentle cynicism to describe the contents of the pulps and summed up by calling Dan Turner, 'the apotheosis of all

private eyes – out of Ma Baker by Dashiell Hammett's Sam Spade.' The article may have surprised Perelman's audience, but none could deny the spicy impact.

Indeed, because Donenfeld and Armer's idea was such a good one, commercially speaking, rival pulps soon began to appear. The Edmar Publishing Company on 45th Street in New York, for example, simply swapped the word 'Spicy' with 'Snappy,' and offered readers tales of *Snappy Detective Mysteries* and *Snappy Romances*.

Snappy Detective Mysteries – 'A Tasty Dish – Nicely Seasoned,' according to its euphemistic shout-line, encompassed sex, horror, and crime in tales like 'Harpy's House' by Frank Kenneth Young ('What nefarious racket

ABOVE
Reginald Greenwood drew illustrations for Snappy Mystery Stories, *including the story of Miss Raffles in 'His Midnight Moll' by Noel Barrow. (June, 1935)*

OPPOSITE
George Quintana was another prolific pulp artist – here illustrating the cover of Snappy Detective Mysteries. *(May, 1935)*

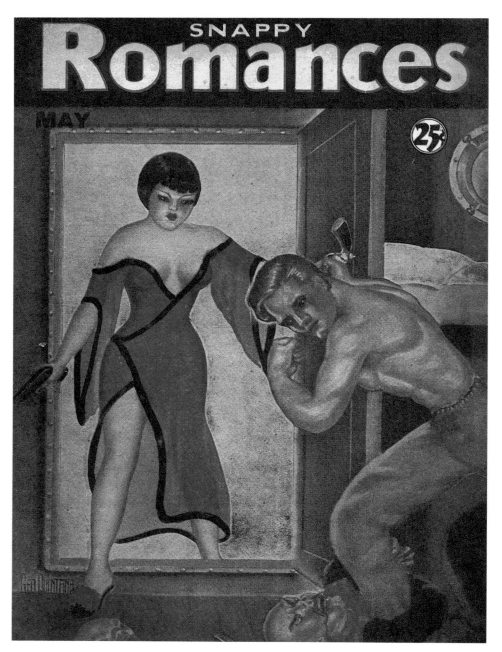

was operated from that secret house of
shame?'), Hamilton Washburn's chiller
'A Dead Man Walks' (' ... and does
things.'), and 'His Midnight Moll' by
Noel Barrow. A novelty in the Barrow
story was the introduction of a female
criminal, interrupted during the course
of a burglary, whose captor knows
precisely how to prevent her escaping:

*'She looked at him, startled. Tony
calmly pointed the automatic at her and
repeated his order. She looked around
her and then, resignedly, began to
loosen the fasteners which she had
snapped shut after the struggle. She
gathered up the torn skirt and slipped
the whole dress over her head, throwing
it to a nearby chair. She stood there
defiantly, a delectable vision of girlish
loveliness, her exquisite figure a
gorgeous symphony of pink and white*

curves, unveiled except for a wispy green brassiere and dainty chiffon panties to match. Tony's admiring eyes swept over the ivory columns of her legs and the gracious swell of her young hips to the perfect breasts and her mutinous face. "Like the show?" she demanded sarcastically ...'

The poor schmuck Tony is, of course, seduced by all this beauty, makes love to the girl ... and wakes up the following morning to find a note on his pillow. It is signed, 'Lady Raffles,' but of the beautiful criminal there is no sign.

Snappy Detective Mysteries carried an outspoken letter's column, 'I Think That,' and ran a large selection of advertisements for sex aids. The main cover artist was George Quintana, who may have lacked the style of H. J. Ward, but was still able to suggest rampant sexuality. The interior artwork was as stylish as that to be found in the Culture magazines, and largely featured the work of Reginald Greenwood, who had an eye-catching way with elegantly posed, dishevelled young girls.

The romance in Snappy Romances – subtitled 'Illustrated Love Fiction' – featured a high percentage of young women slipping out of their clothes more often than they were in them. These girls often proved to be as sexually voracious as the men, and shameless in showing off a lot more than a hint of stocking. A collection of these magazines that recently came on sale in New York was catalogued as having the 'hot parts' marked in purple ink by a former owner who obviously had a penchant for descriptions of the pelvic area. Gives a whole new meaning to the words purple passion!

'Tony's admiring eyes swept over the ivory columns of her legs and the gracious swell of her young hips.'

ABOVE LEFT
Female suffering is featured once again in this anonymous illustration for 'The Decoy' by Edward Earl Lee in Snappy Romances. (September, 1936)

ABOVE RIGHT
No artist took credit for this illustration for Jack Woodford's unintentionally comic story of two calculating females, 'A Pair of Queens' from Snappy Romances. (July, 1936)

ABOVE

This is a typical advertisement from the pages of Snappy Stories. *The book,* Strange Loves, *was being offered for sale in 1936.*

Snappy Romances certainly had a wide range of settings – from the Orient for the story 'Passion Flower,' credited to one 'Okito Seguya,' to South America for 'The Decoy' by Edward Earl Lee, and back home to New York for 'A Pair of Queens' by Jack Woodford, which was actually about two beautiful girls who hunted vulnerable, wealthy young men! The advertisements in this Edmar magazine were also varied, with some for books like *The Merry Order of St. Bridget*, *Tender Bottoms*, and *A Scarlet Pansy* ('The Strange, Exotic World of Twilight Men and Women Revealed!'), plus teasers for 'Sizzling Sexy Photos' and the V-Ray Visualizer – 'By the touch of a magic dial tune in on nudity whenever and wherever you please!' George Quintana provided the cover art, while the pen-and-ink drawings with the stories were virtually all unsigned.

There was no shortage of eroticism to be found in the stories in another pair of mid-30s pulps, *Sizzling Romances* and *Sizzling Detective Mysteries*. They were both launched in 1935 by another New York company, Nudeal Publishing on West 45th Street. *Sizzling Romances* – full of 'Tantalizing Tales,' it informed readers on the contents page – also took readers to far-flung corners of the world that the writers had never been to, if the internal evidence of their texts is anything to go by. Among the classic examples must be Wheeler E. Bell's 'Nipponese Nights' ('What Happened in Old Japan'), 'Oriental Passion' by Joan Baltzar ('A Torrid Tale in a Foreign City'), and 'Drums of Justice' by Nancy Collins ('What the Strange, Beat, Beat, Beat of the Drums Meant to One Woman'). What the drums meant to Atrae Deering, 'a money-mad, gold-digger,' was capture by the local natives and the threat of something terrible:

'Arriving at the charmed circle, the bearers dumped the unconscious, naked woman upon the ground. Shouting with satanic, bacchanalian glee, they danced about her, muttering weird incantations that had dwelt within their breasts down the ages. Thumping with rhythmic, savage insistence the drums beat loudly. Mad with the primeval lust for blood, the natives swarmed upon the woman, their hands clutching at her breasts and thighs. The gods must have a sacrifice. Artae's body arched and fell as the firelight lit every thrust of her agony. Far and near, with a paean of tumultuous ecstasy, the drums of justice invoked a dirge for the Sybarite ...'

The languid cover artwork for *Sizzling Romances* was unsigned, but the interior artwork, consisting primarily of foreign beauties drawn by James Clark, had a certain style.

ABOVE LEFT
*James Clark provided this
Japanese beauty for Wheeler
E. Bell's 'Nipponese Nights' in*
Sizzling Romances. *(July, 1935)*

ABOVE
*The rather languid artwork on the
covers of* Sizzling Romances *belied
the raunchy fiction to be found
inside. (July, 1935)*

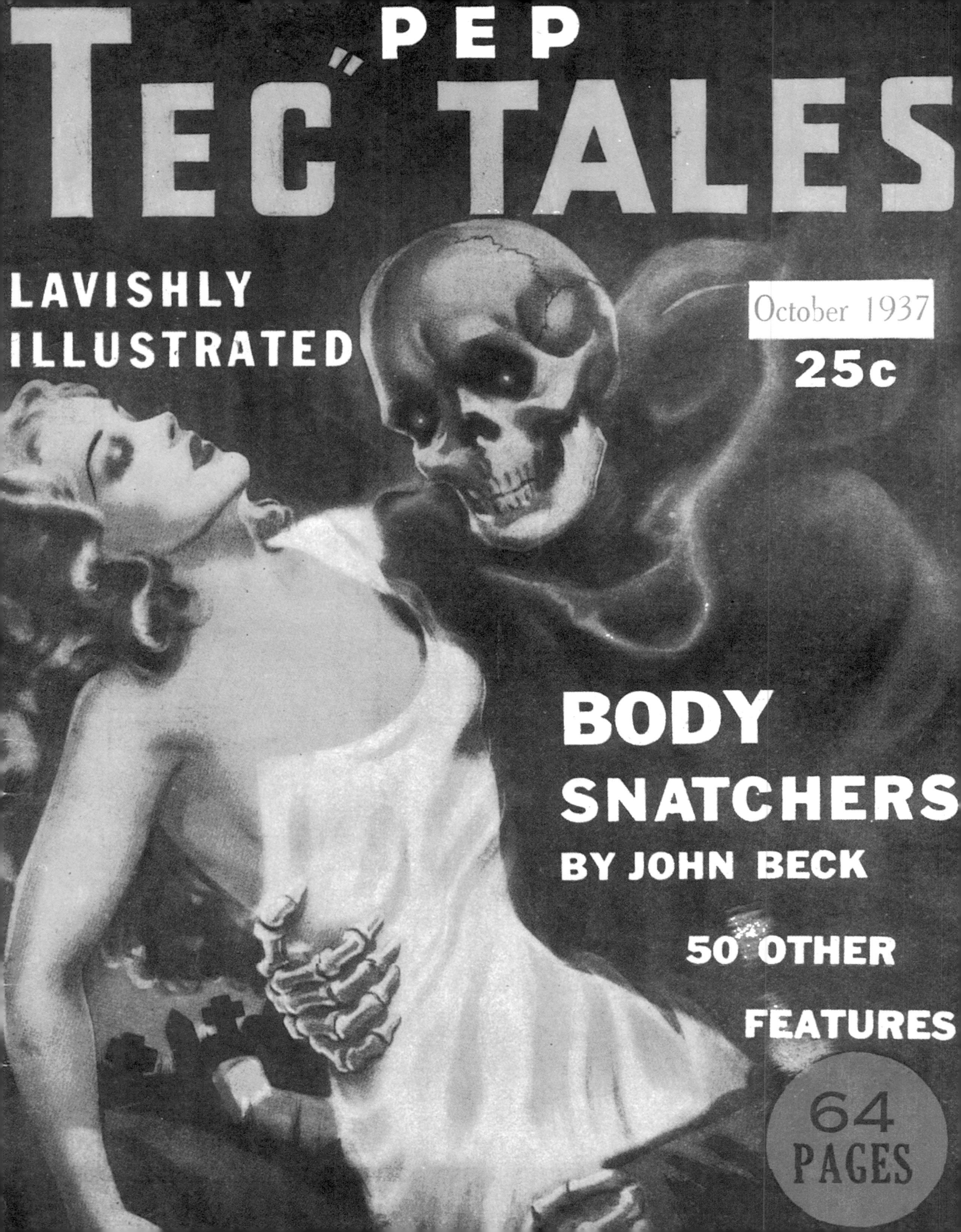
PEP
TEC" TALES
LAVISHLY
ILLUSTRATED
October 1937
25c
BODY
SNATCHERS
BY JOHN BECK
50 OTHER
FEATURES
64
PAGES

The general poor quality of the fiction and the unsigned artwork seemed to suggest the publishers were hedging their bets.

The fiction in Nudeal's other pulp, *Sizzling Detective Mysteries*, was firmly confined within the boundaries of the U.S., the majority of stories taking place in the big cities. 'A Flash in the Dark' by Jerome Wentworth, for example, described a scam in Atlantic City worked by a petty crook, Tim, and his girlfriend, Trixie, which got him shot and her terribly abused by the local mobsters. In Willard Johnston's yarn 'A Woman of Ice,' the teasing Sonia Marinoff fell foul of a gangster and was lucky to escape with her life. In this pulp, too, the cover artist was uncredited, as were most of the interior artists, with the exception of 'L.S.,' who liked to make the most in his illustrations of any *double entendres* he found in the text. 'Manhattan Masquerade' by Gerard Ravel provided one of his best, with a New York artist saying to his nude model, 'It's a little hard, but you'll get used to it.'

Pep Tec Tales was one of the last magazines to cash in on the spicy success. Launched in the fall of 1937 by Graphic Arts Inc. of 501 7th Avenue South, in Minneapolis, the general poor quality of the fiction and the unsigned artwork seemed to suggest the publishers were hedging their bets. Even an attempt to run a two-page spread of suggestive jokes, with offers of cash to readers for more funnies, was less than successful. It is probably true to say that the publishers already realized that the end was near for this particular pulp gravy train, and the whole idea was, of course, no longer new. Equally, the pressures of

ABOVE

Even gruesome illustrations, such as this one for 'The Chemise Murders' by Norman A. Daniels, failed to prevent the demise of Pep Tec Tales. *(November, 1937)*

OPPOSITE

Pep Tec Tales *was a poor relation of the spicy pulps and did not last long, despite the classic cover combination of beauty and violence. (October, 1937)*

PEP TEC

The
*PAJAMA
PARTY
KILLER*

*By
DON
LAWRENCE.*

JUNE
25
CENTS

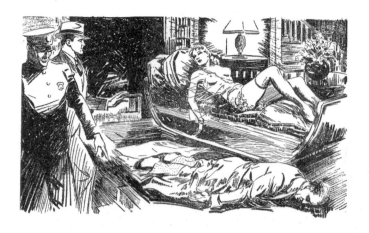

Playboy Jud Burwell joins the Vice Squad for a thrill 'and gets it when he sets a trap for kidnappers with his own life for bait.'

censorship had been increasing on all the hot magazines, and several companies had been taken to court with punitive results. As one commentator remarked, 'Nudity was now being cut out and the bras were going back on.'

Even the suggestiveness of the *Pep Tec Tales* copywriter could not disguise its failings. 'The Chemise Murders' by Norman A. Daniels was lamely introduced as 'A woman-hating detective and a brave girl clash with a murderer whose grisly killings have baffled the police,' while Edmond Beville's 'The Curse of the Rusty Roses'

featured playboy Jud Burwell, who joins the Vice Squad for a thrill, 'and gets it when he sets a trap for kidnappers with his own life for bait.' The title story of the June 1937 issue, 'The Pajama Party Killer' by Don Lawrence, had an even more apt subtitle. The story described the discovery of an unconscious prostitute beside the corpse of a leading New York broker following an all-night orgy. Beneath the picture of the scene ran the caption, 'A midnight murder put the Joy Girl behind bars. What future for her now?' It was perhaps a fitting epitaph for the spicy pulps, too.

ABOVE
This unsigned illustration for Don Lawrence's story of 'The Pajama Party Killer' is from Pep Tec Tales. *(June, 1938)*

OPPOSITE
This was an oddity among hot pulp covers – the significance of the girl breaking an egg on her iron must have puzzled readers of Pep Tec. *(June, 1938)*

The Naked *and* the Dead

THE FANTASY PULPS

Clark Henneberger had a dual interest in Edgar Allan Poe and smutty jokes – the kind college students enjoy telling one another.

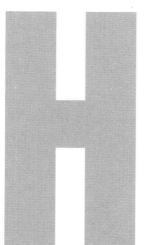

enneberger was born in the last decade of the 19th century, and was a 16-year-old student at a military academy in Virginia when he discovered the works of the master of horror. To use Henneberger's own expression, he became 'immersed in Poe,' and decided that he, too, wanted to become a writer. To further this objective he worked on several newspapers before fate led him to Indianapolis. Here he was to have the idea that would ultimately result in him being acknowledged as one of the great publishers of weird fiction. Initially, though, his plan was to run a magazine for students.

The Collegiate World, which Henneberger launched in 1919, was uninspired, dull, and it flopped. Undeterred, however, Henneberger relaunched the magazine as *College Humor*, packed it with jokes and suggestive illustrations, and this time had

CO-ED CARNIVAL!

FOTOS, FICTION
FUN AND
FASHIONS IN

COLLEGE HUMOR

THE SMARTEST
COMEDY IN AMERICA

NOW 15c AT ALL
ON SALE STANDS

BEST
ARTICLES
ON SPORT
EVERY
ISSUE

ABOVE

This is an advertisement for College Humor, *the magazine that helped Clark Henneberger to establish his publishing empire.*

OPPOSITE

This brilliant cover for Weird Tales *by Margaret Brundage illustrates the Robert E. Howard story,* 'Black Colossus.' *(June, 1933)*

an overnight success on his hands. Within three years he had added several other titles to his burgeoning empire, including *The Magazine of Fun* and two other publications of which little is known beyond the fact they were 'semipornographic.' The real surprise came in 1922, when Henneberger set up Rural Publications Inc. in the Baldwin Building, Indianapolis, and announced his intention of launching a magazine called *Weird Tales*. It would be a repository for the kind of stories Edgar Allan Poe had written, he said, and no one suspected that he was about to give birth to arguably the most famous pulp of all.

Henneberger started *Weird Tales* because he appreciated there was no outlet for authors who wanted to write stories of fantasy and horror. He also decided to set certain standards for quality fiction which, in the fullness of time, would produce some of the greatest American weird story writers of the 20th century, including H. P. Lovecraft, Seabury Quinn, Clark Ashton Smith, Robert E. Howard, Robert Bloch, and Ray Bradbury. The first issue, subtitled 'The Unique Magazine,' was edited by Henneberger's appointee Edwin Baird and appeared in March 1923, but without any fanfare and to no particular acclaim. A year later, and Henneberger's dream seemed

as if it would fare no better than *The Collegiate World*. But a bumper issue for May/July 1924 changed all that when it ran a story, 'The Loved Dead' by C. M. Eddy, which had been revised for publication by H. P. Lovecraft. It was a tale about necrophilia, and so controversial in style and descriptiveness that copies of *Weird Tales* had to be withdrawn from sale in many places. Within days, the magazine had become a *cause célèbre*, and any surviving copies were immediately snapped up.

In the aftermath of this furore, Henneberger decided to persevere with *Weird Tales*. He looked for a new editor – trying unsuccessfully to talk Lovecraft into the job – but ultimately settled on a member of his own staff, Farnsworth Wright, who, in the years that followed, maintained the magazine's literary standing although he never quite made it achieve the financial stability it deserved. That same year of 1924, the publisher's name was changed to Popular Fiction Publishing Co. and the editorial offices were moved to Chicago, a city with which the magazine has remained forever associated. Later, *Weird Tales* would be relocated a third time to New York, where it continued to be published until the final issue, number 279, appeared in September 1954.

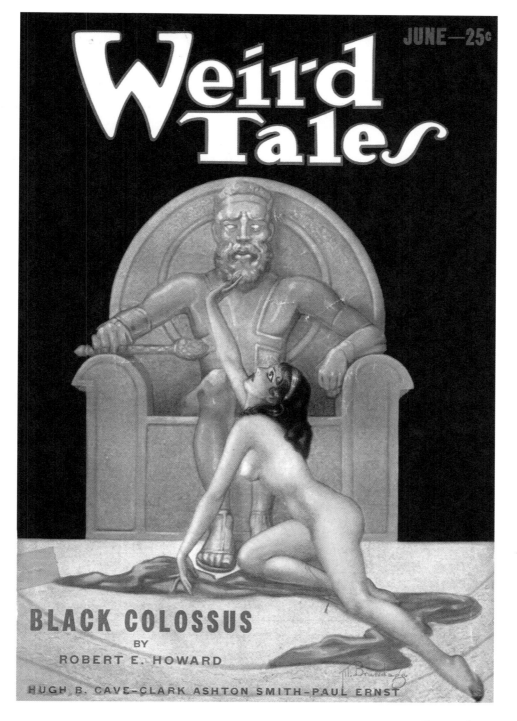

It was a tale about necrophilia, and so controversial in style and descriptiveness that copies of *Weird Tales* had to be withdrawn from sale in many places.

Aside from its roll call of classic authors, *Weird Tales* is also deservedly famous for its cover art – especially the colorful nude extravagances of a Chicago housewife named Margaret Brundage, who made her debut in the September 1932 issue. Her name is now virtually synonymous with that of the magazine in the minds of readers and admirers all over the world. Henneberger, of course, had never made any secret of his liking for a little smut, and undraped females appeared in the pulp's pages almost from the first issue. The main contributor of these illustrations was Hugh Rankin, who joined the *Weird Tales* team in the mid-20s. He worked with a grease pencil on textured board to provide pictures that had a unique dreamlike quality and made his nudes even more alluring. Rankin provided interior art for some of the greatest stories by Lovecraft ('The Call of Cthulhu'), Howard ('The People of the Black Circle'), and Hoffmann Price ('The Tarbis of the Lake').

Margaret Brundage had attended the Chicago Academy of Fine Arts and trained as a fashion artist. When she found work hard to come by because of the Depression – and with a young child and an aged mother to support – she approached *Weird Tales*.

Brundage and the magazine were made for each other, and readers were soon writing in enthusiastically about her work. To those who asked, the artist readily explained how she worked. After reading the original manuscript of a story, she would submit some sample sketches and when one had been selected by Farnsworth Wright, she would complete the final picture on canvas with pastel chalks. On one occasion she commented, 'They would always pick the one that showed a girl with the least amount of clothing – they felt that those were the best for the covers and sold most copies.'

Brundage's ability to depict stunning beauty and strong sensuality was particularly evident in one picture illustrating Robert E. Howard's story 'Black Colossus' in the June 1933 issue. This, according to the editor writing in his column 'The Eyrie,' produced more fan mail than any other cover, and was also the author's own favorite

Henneberger had never made any secret of his liking for a little smut, and undraped females appeared in the pulp's pages almost from the first issue.

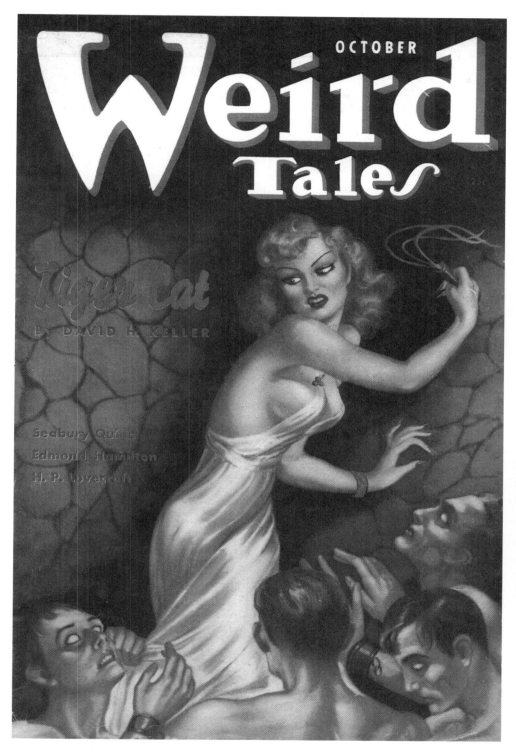

ABOVE

This classic whipping scene by Margaret Brundage illustrates 'Tiger Cat' by David R. Keller on the cover of Weird Tales. (October, 1937)

RIGHT TOP

Featured in Weird Tales, this is one of Hugh Rankin's fine grease pencil on textured board illustrations for 'The Curse of the Valedi' by S. P. Meek. (July, 1935)

ABOVE

Ed Whitham provided this modest illustration for H. P. Lovecraft's fine story 'The Moon-Bog,' which appeared in Weird Tales. (January, 1926)

ABOVE

Virgil Finlay provided the illustrations for 'The Tree of Life' by C. L. Moore in Weird Tales. *(October, 1936)*

RIGHT

This exquisite nude was created by Virgil Finlay for Weird Tales. *(February, 1938)*

illustration for one of his stories. She also did a number of covers featuring the work of Seabury Quinn – notably for his story 'Satan's Palimpsest' – and was amused by the fact that Quinn always included an erotic nude scene in his tales because he knew there was a good chance that Wright would ask Brundage to illustrate it on the cover! Such promotion may have helped Seabury Quinn to become the most popular author in *Weird Tales*, despite the competition from Lovecraft et al. Margaret Brundage was the first of the pulp's artists to feature torture – in her case a whipping scene for Robert E. Howard's 'The Slithering Shadow' in September 1933. Her best picture of this kind is generally agreed to be the one for 'Tiger Cat' by David R. Keller on the front of *Weird Tales*, October 1937. All of these pictures got readers in quite a lather, especially Forrest J. Ackerman of Hollywood, who was then starting to collect his famous archive of sci-fi and fantasy material. He wrote to the editor in November 1935:

'As far back as I can remember, your covers have featured unclad heroines. Your contention seems to be, "Clothes make the woman – ordinary!" Yesteryear, your covers were not so controversial because, though nude, the hapless heroines were more vaguely, indistinctly illustrated. Then came the Brundage beauties, in all their curvy clarity! Reader Robson in your September issue, sums up for the opposition in what I should hazard will become a famous phrase, "After all, the thrill of viewing a nude isn't exactly a weird one." Ponder that!'

At this same period, another brilliantly individualistic artist was making his presence felt inside *Weird Tales*, and would soon burst out in glorious flesh tints all over the covers. His name was Virgil Finlay, and his fame was destined to spread far beyond the confines of the pulp. Finlay was born in Rochester, New York. He revealed a natural ability as an artist in his teens and took a course at night school to develop this talent. He was an avid reader of the pulp magazines and became convinced he could do as well, if not better, than those who were illustrating them. Finlay loved fantasy stories, and where better to send some sample artwork than *Weird Tales*? He was just 21 years old when Farnsworth Wright bought and published his first picture of a reclining nude with the head of Medusa. Thereafter, he became a favorite with readers and, like Margaret Brundage, provided illustrations for a number of the pulp's best-known authors, especially H. P. Lovecraft, with whom he became friendly.

Virgil Finlay's work was constantly inventive and experimental, but he undoubtedly made his mark on *Weird Tales* with his nude figures for the covers of issues like that of February 1938 featuring Seabury Quinn's tale of the 'Frozen Beauty.' When drawing interior art, Finlay came closer to the full frontal nude than any previous artist, in his illustrations for 'The Tree of Life' by C. L. Moore (October, 1936),

'As far back as I can remember, your covers have featured unclad heroines.'

and the curious figure for 'Living Buddhess' by Seabury Quinn (November 1937), which surely answered the question posed by 'Reader Robson' about nudes and the weird! At this stage in his career, Finlay had not yet resorted to covering the delicate parts of the female anatomy with the stars and bubbles that would become the hallmark of his later work when contributing to other magazines, such as *Famous Fantastic Mysteries*, of which more later.

Among the hundreds of letters written to *Weird Tales* by readers, one received in April 1938 from Robert W. Lowndes of Greenwich, Connecticut – who was to become a pulp editor and writer nicknamed 'Doc' Lowndes – can be taken as typical of a great many more:

ABOVE

This bizarre image of a bound female body was one of Virgil Finlay's most unforgettable creations for Weird Tales. *(November, 1937)*

'The artwork in the February issue of *Weird Tales* leaves one rather breathless, a delight heightened for me by the fact that, after four days tirelessly haunting local newsstands, gnawing my nails at the thought that the magazine might have been suspended, a copy shone there, today, before my still-hopeful eyes, in all its radiant glory. Virgil Finlay's creation is real and gorgeously vibrant with the illusion of actuality. And the male figure, with its proper expression of adoration, is no less commendable. As for his black and white work, I still fail to see signs of deterioration, which might be expected, in as much as Finlay is doing the lion's share of the drawings.'

In fact, Lowndes's difficulty in obtaining a copy of the February 1938 issue was a hint of things to come. For in late 1938, *Weird Tales* was sold to Short Stories Inc., and moved to Rockefeller Plaza, in New York. There it almost immediately suffered from a campaign by the mayor against the displaying of sensational pulp magazine covers on newsstands. This necessitated a change of policy by the new editor, Dorothy McIlwraith – no more nudes would grace the magazine. But the passing of Brundage and Finlay did not mean the end of 'girlie art' in *Weird Tales* – just the beginning of a different

LEFT

The Weird Tales *Thorp McClusky story, 'The Haunted Hour,' was illustrated by another unique Hannes Bok creation. (July, 1946)*

fantasy writer, Abraham Merritt. When some of Bok's work came to the notice of *Weird Tales* contributors, the author Ray Bradbury promptly recommended him to the magazine. The young man's flamboyant and exotic style was ideally suited to the pulp and he was invited to join the team of artists. Covers like that for the March 1940 issue, which had an elfin beauty illustrating Clyde Irvine's tale of 'The Horror of the Glen,' and the robust, unashamed interior nude for 'Haunted Hour' by Thorp McClusky in 1946, revealed a unique talent. Bok said his object was to create 'kodachromes of the impossible.' And among those who praised his work was none other than his champion, Ray Bradbury, who wrote from Los Angeles in 1940:

'Today is the day of days for me, for I have just been to the newsstand and bought my copy of *Weird Tales* with the cover excellently painted by Hannes

type. Two artists in particular were to carry on the standard – Hannes Bok and Lee Brown Coye.

Bok was a young, Seattle-born artist who had never been formally trained as an illustrator, but was inspired by the art of the great Maxfield Parrish and the

ABOVE

This wonderful Hannes Bok cover illustration was for 'The Horror of the Glen' by Clyde Irvine, for Weird Tales. *(March, 1940)*

Females were often seen at the mercy of the most bizarre forms of human (and inhuman) beings.

Bok. I have waited patiently for years to see Bok do a *Weird Tales* cover – and now the day has come. I can only say that Bok shows a wonderful ability in this debut. His coloring sense surpasses Finlay and, given future chances at the cover, he will, I have no doubt, give Virgil a run for his money. I only hope the rest of the fan world backs me upon this for Hannes is a master at portraying symphonies in color. *Weird Tales* needs an artist with such an imagination.'

In spite of this praise, Hannes Bok struggled to make a living from his art, and it was not until after his death that he earned the recognition he deserved, when some admirers set up the 'Bokanalia Foundation' to preserve his unique work.

Lee Brown Coye, on the other hand, made a similar impact in the pages of *Weird Tales*, and after the demise of the magazine, went on to produce art and covers for numerous fantasy book publishers, especially Arkham House, which issued a number of books by *Weird Tales* contributors. Described as 'a master of the weird and grotesque,' Coye provided the interior art for numerous short stories and for a series entitled 'Weirdisms' about the lore and legend of the supernatural. In this, females were often seen at the mercy of the most bizarre forms of human (and inhuman) beings. He also had the distinction of creating the cover for the March 1948 issue of *Weird Tales* to commemorate the magazine's 25th anniversary. It was a landmark date that no horror pulp – and few other pulps – would come anywhere near equalling.

The first pulp to follow the example set by *Weird Tales* was *Ghost Stories*, launched in July 1926 by New York entrepreneur Bernarr Macfadden, boss of Constructive Publishing, Broadway. As the title suggests, it carried only ghost stories: a mixture of 'true

ABOVE LEFT
This unmistakable Lee Brown Coye illustration was for the Weird Tales *series 'Weirdisms.' (July, 1951)*

OPPOSITE
Lee Brown Coye also painted this cover, for the 25th Anniversary issue of Weird Tales. *(March, 1948)*

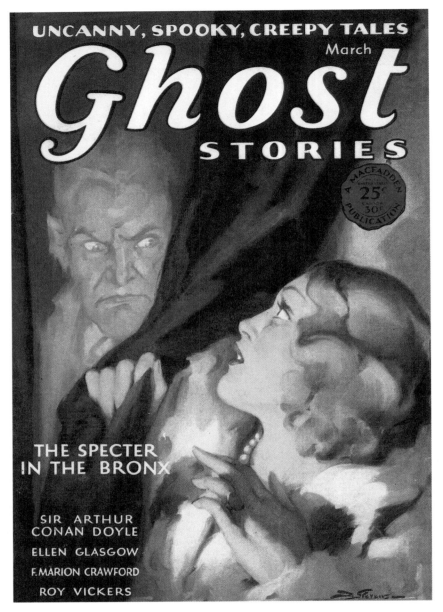

UNCANNY, SPOOKY, CREEPY TALES

March

Ghost

STORIES

A MACFADDEN PUBLICATION

25¢

THE SPECTER
IN THE BRONX

SIR ARTHUR
CONAN DOYLE

ELLEN GLASGOW

F. MARION CRAWFORD

ROY VICKERS

LEFT

*Dalton Stevens
developed a real
skill for picturing the
supernatural on his
covers for* Ghost
Stories. *(March, 1930)*

BELOW

*An artist signing
himself with the single
letter 'E' provided most
of the interior artwork
for* Ghost Stories, *like
this example for 'Did
This Man Have
Two Bodies?'
(November 1928)*

experiences' usually written by the editor, Harry A. Keller, or a member of his staff; reprints of classic supernatural stories; and occasionally original tales by writers like Ray Cummings, Hugh B. Cave, Victor Rousseau, and Robert E. Howard. The magazine had a curious policy of using photographs of specially posed models to illustrate many of the contributions, plus the occasional line decoration. Only the covers painted by Dalton Stevens, who endeavored to make his ghosts look realistic rather than ridiculous, were of any quality. *Ghost Stories*, though, thrived for 64 issues until 1931.

Tales of Magic and Mystery, which hit the newsstands in December 1927, was a more straightforward magazine, published by the Personal Arts Company of Camden, in New Jersey. Edited by Walter Gibson, the pulp had a particular yen for stories of the occult – both true and fictional. In its short run of just two years, *Tales of Magic and Mystery* carried stories by a number of

The magazine had a curious policy of using photographs of specially posed models to illustrate many of the contributions.

the big names in horror fiction including Frank Owen ('The Black Well of Wadi'), Miriam Allen deFord ('Ghostly Hands'), H. P. Lovecraft ('Cool Air'), and the indefatigable Robert Leslie Bellem ('The Flowers of Enchantment'). The occult expert Howard Thurston contributed a monthly article on his experiences, and other articles covered topics as varied as Houdini and the 'evil eye' of superstition. There has been some debate as to who the pulp's stylish cover artist was, but the consensus of opinion points to Earle Bergey.

Strange Tales, which appeared in September 1931, was a much more direct rival to *Weird Tales*, and was produced in New York by the Clayton magazine group. Legend has it that the

company president, William Clayton, suddenly found he had a gap in his monthly production schedule for magazine covers, and asked his managing editor, Harry Bates, to fill this with a horror title. *Strange Tales* was

ABOVE
The versatile Earle Bergey is believed to have created this impressionist cover for Tales of Magic and Mystery. *(March, 1928)*

LEFT

This is another of H. W. Wesso's compelling covers, for 'Wolves of Darkness' by Jack Williamson in Strange Tales. *(June, 1932)*

ABOVE

Earle Bergey was responsible for this superb Strange Tales *cover illustrating John Clemons's story 'The Panting Beast.' (June, 1940)*

The stories had a strong flavor of action and adventure well laced with vampires, mummies, zombis, and black magic.

ABOVE

An Amos Sewell illustration of Conan for the Robert E. Howard story 'People of the Dark' in Strange Tales. *(June, 1932)*

the outcome, and it was soon attracting a number of *Weird Tales* authors with offers of higher pay – Robert E. Howard ('People of the Dark'), Clark Ashton Smith ('The Hunters From Beyond'), and Ray Cummings ('The Dead Who Walk') to name just three. The stories had a strong flavor of action and adventure well laced with vampires, mummies, zombis, and black magic. There were also short articles on supernatural topics, and a correspondence column for readers called 'The Cauldron – A Meeting Place for Sorcerers and Apprentices.' The interior artwork varied from the excellent to the mediocre, the most notable contributors being Amos Sewell, Rafael De Soto, and B. B. Alexander. The covers were the sole preserve of the Polish émigré Hans Waldemar Wessolowksi, who signed his pictures

LEFT

Cover artist Rafael De Soto also drew interior illustrations, such as this one for 'The House in the Magnolias' by Derleth and Schorer from Strange Tales. *(June, 1932)*

'H. W. Wesso.' His cover for the January 1932 issue, 'Wolves of Darkness' by Jack Williamson, is a classic. Sadly, a year later, and after just seven issues of the pulp had been released, the Clayton empire collapsed, and all Harry Bates's hard work in trying to outsell *Weird Tales* came to nothing – although the name of *Strange Tales* is still held in high regard.

The similarly titled *Strange Stories*, launched in February 1939 from Ned Pines' Better Publications Inc., also managed to survive only for 13 issues of bimonthly publication. It was visualized as a companion to the company's various 'Thrilling' titles, including *Thrilling Mystery* and *Thrilling Wonder Stories*, although editor Mort Weisinger said he was aiming for 'more shocks.' To achieve this he drew on the *Weird Tales* roster of writers, including Robert

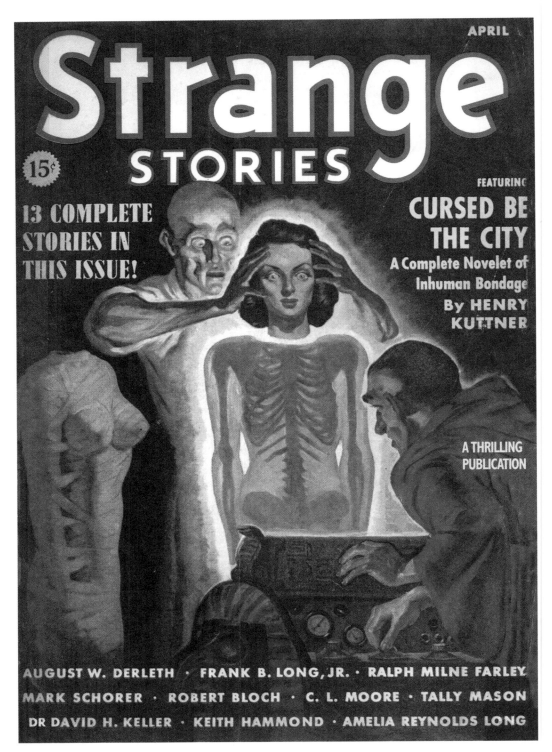

LEFT

Rudolph Belarski was at his imaginative best for 'Cursed Be The City' by Henry Kuttner on the cover of Strange Stories. *(April, 1939)*

ABOVE LEFT

Far-flung locations were a favorite of Robert Gibson Jones when illustrating stories for Fantastic Adventures, *such as 'The Court of Kublai Khan' by David V. Reed. (March, 1948)*

Strange Stories might well have threatened the popularity of 'The Unique Magazine,' especially because it kept its price tag at 5 cents below that of its rival and was given a special sales push across the nation at the very time when *Weird Tales* was suffering a drop in sales. The reason for its failure has remained a mystery, although it has been suggested that the decision of Mort Weisinger to leave the editorial chair (he went off to edit *Superman*) may have been instrumental. Certainly, copies of the pulp, with its eye-catching covers and plethora of stories that later became anthology favorites, are as enthusiastically sought by collectors today as those of *Weird Tales*.

Fantastic Adventures was the next pulp to seek the nickels and dimes of horror fans. It was launched in May 1939, by the Ziff-Davis Publishing Company of 608 South Dearborn Street in Chicago, as a companion to their sci-fi pulp, *Amazing Stories*. Edited by B. G. Davis, it offered a mix of supernatural fiction, lost race adventures, and even a little science fiction, with contributing authors that included Robert Bloch, Ray Bradbury, and August Derleth, plus the occasional short story by Edgar Rice Burroughs,

Bloch ('Death Has Five Guesses'), August W. Derleth ('Logoda's Heads'), and Henry Kuttner ('Cursed Be The City', billed as 'A complete novelette of inhuman bondage'). There was also a regular column, 'The Black Arts' by 'Lucifer' – apparently a 'Famous Authority on Witchcraft and Black Magic.' With evocative cover artwork by Earle Bergey and Rudolph Belarski, plus interior illustrations by Leo Morey, Alex Schomburg, and Virgil Finlay,

ABOVE

This is another of Belarski's gruesome pictorial creations for a cover of Strange Stories. *(June, 1939)*

including 'The Scientists Revolt,' which appeared in the second issue. Among the features was a long-running series of 'Fantastic Hoaxes' written by Julius Schwartz and illustrated by Joe Sewell, and a full-color back-page illustration drawn by Frank R. Paul visualizing the inhabitants on other planets. The front cover art was shared between Leo Morey, H. W. McCauley, and Robert Gibson Jones, who was especially good at historical scenes, while the rather stylized interior work was provided by Julian Krupa, Jay Jackson, and Robert Fuqua.

The Ziff-Davis pulp continued for 128 issues until 1951. The following year it became a digest-size magazine with an abbreviated title, *Fantastic*, and a new editor, Howard Browne, who concentrated solely on tales of fantasy during the 30 years of its subsequent successful existence. The magazine not only presented long-time favorites, such as Ray Bradbury and Cornell Woolrich, but nurtured new talents including Harlan Ellison, John Jakes, and Michael Moorcock, not to mention discovering a number of unlikely authors who had written stories of fantasy: Truman Capote, Raymond Chandler, Evelyn Waugh, and even Mickey Spillane. Browne also demanded – and got – a high standard of artwork for *Fantastic*, with Rupert Conrad supplying a rich selection of voluptuous, near-naked females for the covers, and 'Ed Emsh' (short for Edward Emshwiller) doing much the same inside – notably for Mickey Spillane's tale of 'The Veiled Woman.' However, the magazine's claim that it was

'profusely illustrated in color by leading artists' was stretching the truth a little far, as the color amounted to no more than a single tint on any picture!

Unknown is the pulp that can be seen, in hindsight, to have been almost as influential as *Weird Tales*. It emerged from Street & Smith in March 1939 and, in a total of 38 issues, probably published more quality fantasy per issue than any other pulp. Indeed, it has been credited with acquiring a respectability for fantasy among readers that the genre had not enjoyed for years. The success of *Unknown* owed much to the

Unknown probably published more quality fantasy per issue than any other pulp.

ABOVE

This is one of Fantastic's *'colored' illustrations by Ed Emsh for 'The Veiled Woman' by Mickey Spillane. (November/December, 1952)*

GREAT NEW STORIES OF FANTASY AND SCIENCE FICTION!
William P. McGivern • Ralph Robin • John Wyndham • others

ABOVE

Rupert Conrad kept up the high standard of covers for Fantasy *when the magazine went digest size. (July/August, 1953)*

ABOVE RIGHT

This truly weird cover by H. W. Scott for Unknown *illustrated Norvell W. Page's Oriental epic 'Flame Winds.' (June, 1939)*

editorial acumen of John W. Campbell, who had been in charge of Street & Smith's *Astounding Science Fiction*, and was looking for a vehicle in which to publish the excellent stories he was receiving that did not fit into the category of sci-fi. What was new about much of this fiction was its attempt to treat the supernatural as a kind of science operating under its own laws. The idea caught on with pulp readers and was brilliantly developed in stories by Robert Heinlein ('The Devil Makes the Law') and Jack Williamson ('Darker Than You Think'), and also in Fritz Leiber's tale of witchcraft at work in a modern setting ('Conjure Wife'). Other authors who contributed tales like this included Eric Frank Russell, Theodore Sturgeon, and L. Sprague de Camp.

Tragically, *Unknown* was cancelled by Street & Smith during the Second World War in order to ensure enough paper for *Astounding*. But this was not before it had left an important mark on pulp history in general, and fantasy fiction in particular, that makes it worthy of comparison with *Weird Tales*. H. W. Scott was responsible for the most innovative of the *Unknown* covers, while inside Edd Cartier set a standard with his whimsical, sensual, and always eye-catching drawings, which earned him an enviable reputation among both readers and other illustrators.

What was new about much of this fiction was its attempt to treat the supernatural as a kind of science operating under its own laws.

Another pulp of this era, also famed for its artwork, was *Famous Fantastic Mysteries*. It came from pulp pioneer Frank Munsey's empire. Initially, the magazine reprinted stories from the company's earlier pulps – *All-Story Weekly*, *Argosy*, and *Cavalier* – but when it was later taken over by Popular Publications in March 1943, and edited by Mary Gnaedinger, it began to include short stories by writers of the ilk of Ray Bradbury, Henry Kuttner, and C. L. Moore, plus novels by a number of overseas authors whose work was still largely unknown in the U.S., including a trio of English writers,

E. F. Benson, Algernon Blackwood, and William Hope Hodgson. There were even some surprising reprints in *Famous Fantastic Mysteries* of stories by C. S. Forester, Ayn Rand, and Franz Kafka.

The pulp was also well served by its two great illustrators: the ex-*Weird Tales* star, Virgil Finlay, and Lawrence Sterne Stevens, who at his best was every bit the equal of his colleague. Occasionally, the cover work of the two men was almost indistinguishable – though inside the pulp it was the stars and bubbles that Finlay had adopted for modesty's sake that gave his identity away. Both men were

ABOVE LEFT

Edd Cartier created this beautiful knight for 'The Mathematics of Magic' by Sprague de Camp and Fletcher Pratt in Unknown. *(August, 1940)*

ABOVE RIGHT

Modest bubbles replace stars on Finlay's cover for another Merritt classic, 'Creep, Shadow!' in Famous Fantastic Mysteries. *(August, 1942)*

unsurpassable at picturing female beauty, as Finlay demonstrated on covers for two of A. Merritt's classic fantasies, 'Burn, Witch, Burn!' (June 1942) and 'Creep, Shadow!' (August 1942), and which Stevens matched – without the pyrotechnics – for 'The Island of Captain Sparrow' by S. Fowler Wright (April 1946) and Jack London's end-of-the-world novel, 'The Scarlet Plague' (February 1949). Once again, it is true to say that these magazines are collected today more for their illustrations than for the stories that they contain.

The Second World War effectively marked the end of the great horror pulps, as it did for so many of these magazines. *Weird Tales*, of course, continued, and Popular Publications, which had taken over *Famous Fantastic Mysteries*, had a brief try in 1949 at cashing in on the continuing interest in the tales of Abraham Merritt. It launched a magazine solely devoted to

his work, *A. Merritt's Fantasy Magazine*, edited by Mary Gnaedinger. Predictably, the publisher soon ran out of fiction by the master and, even bolstered with short stories by Ray Cummings, Victor Rousseau, Eric North, and Jack Williamson, the magazine did not survive beyond five issues, ceasing publication in October 1950. Virgil Finlay's illustrations from the previous publication of the Merritt stories were reprinted inside the magazine, while Norman Saunders was well below his best with a series of rather uninspired covers.

Memories of the great days of the horror pulps were kept alive for a

ABOVE LEFT

This is another of Lawrence Stevens's excellent covers for Famous Fantastic Mysteries, *depicting Jack London's fantasy classic, 'The Scarlet Plague.' (February, 1949)*

ABOVE RIGHT

Lawrence Stevens liked to use natural items to preserve the modesty of his naked females – this example, from 'Rebirth' by Thomas Calvert McClary, appeared in Famous Fantastic Mysteries. *(October, 1951)*

OPPOSITE

Lawrence Stevens created high-quality covers for Famous Fantastic Mysteries, *like this one for 'The Island of Captain Sparrow' by S. Fowler Wright. (April, 1946)*

In truth though, the stories in *True Weird* were never really horrifying, none of the monsters were very frightening, and all the damsels in distress were now decently clothed.

while by a small group of digest-size magazines. Notable among these was the *Avon Fantasy Reader* (1947–52), published by the Avon Book Co. of 119 West 57th Street, New York. Edited by Donald A. Wollheim, who would later become the publisher of the fantasy paperback imprint, DAW Books, it carried reprints by classic writers including M. R. James, H. G. Wells, and Lord Dunsany alongside more recent work by Lovecraft, Howard, and Bradbury. Although there was no interior artwork, the 18 issues of the *Avon Fantasy Reader* were all enhanced with gaudy covers in the best traditions of the old-style pulps, several the work of Bernard Barton. *Fantasy Magazine* (1953–54), from Future Publications of 175 Fifth Avenue, edited by Lester del Rey, lasted an even shorter period, despite carrying 'all-new stories' by Robert Sheckley ('The Demons'), Philip K. Dick ('The Cookie Lady'), and England's John Wyndham ('More Spinned Against'), as well as excellent artwork by Hannes Bok and Ed Emsh.

The last of this group, *True Weird* (1955–56), from Weider Periodicals in Jersey City, was edited by Howard Booth, and for several issues was published in standard pulp format, before dropping down to digest size.

It set out to mix fiction in the *Weird Tales* tradition with allegedly true stories of horror from around the world – for example, 'When The Vampire Was Captured' by Ward Semple, 'The Floating Bejeweled Hand' by Paul Harris, and 'Fish With Human Hands Attacked Me' by Arthur A. Dunn, all presented in a kind of pseudo-*National Enquirer* style. The interior artwork was provided by a team of artists including Dwight Howe, George Paine, and Warren Knight – their illustrations were frequently augmented with photographs and maps – while the covers were handled by Clarence Doore. In truth though, the stories in *True Weird* were never really horrifying, none of the monsters were very frightening, and all the damsels in distress were now decently clothed. *True Weird* was a far cry indeed from the images of the naked and the dead, which had founded the 'weird' tradition back in the heyday of *Weird Tales* all those years before.

BELOW
This cover by Clarence Doore was for one of the last of the horror pulps, True Weird. *(November, 1955)*

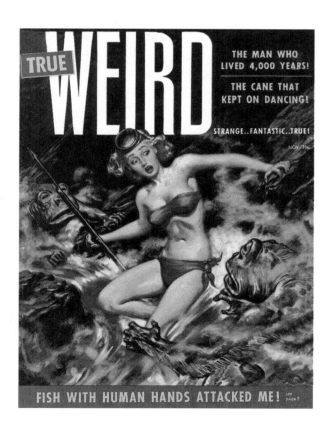

OPPOSITE LEFT
The prolific Norman Saunders was the main cover artist for the short-lived A. Merritt's Fantasy Magazine. *(July, 1950)*

OPPOSITE RIGHT
Bernard Barton painted the best of Avon Fantasy Reader's *covers, like this one for Robert E. Howard's 'The Blonde Goddess of Bal-Sagoth.' (Winter, 1950)*

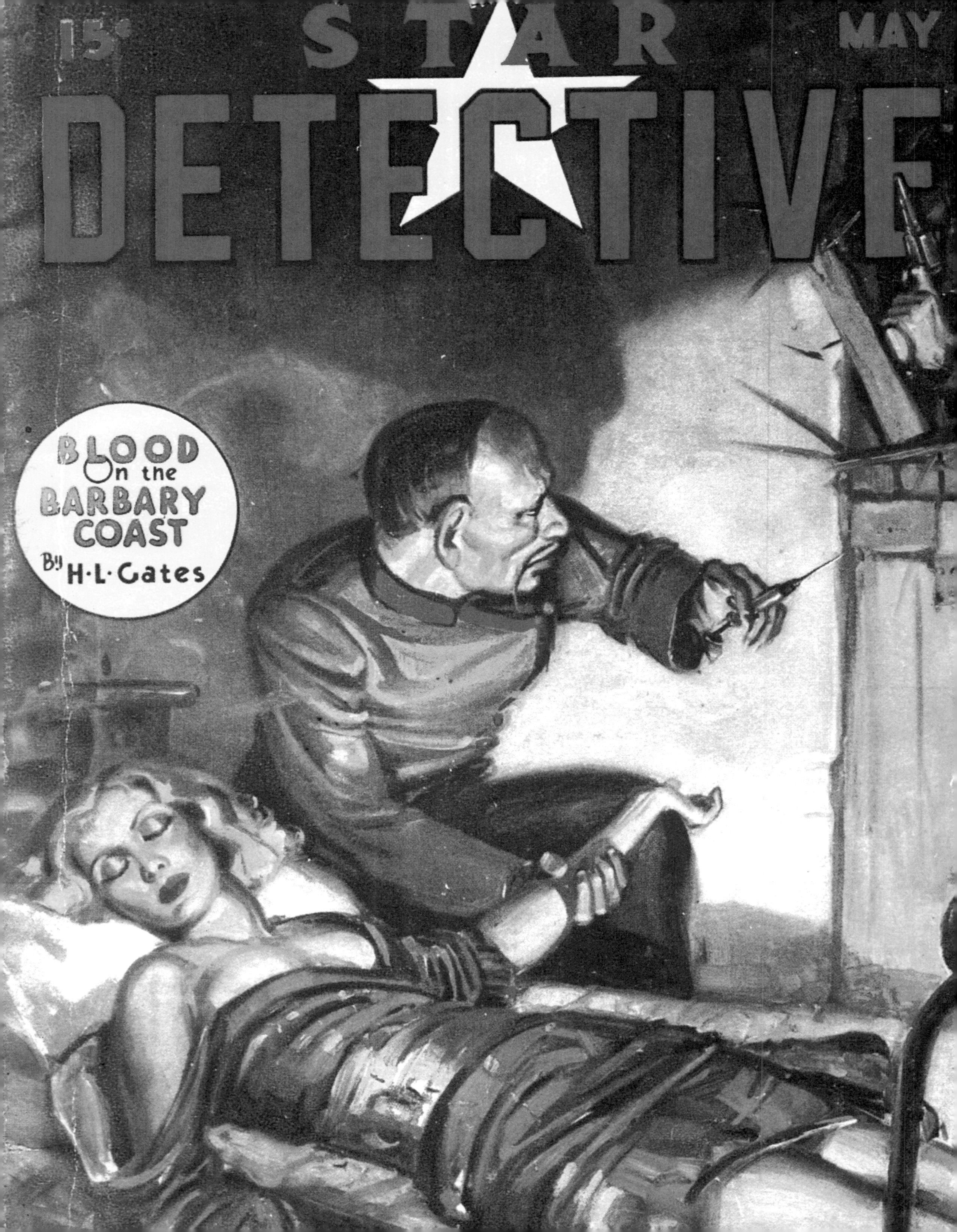
15¢
STAR
DETECTIVE
MAY
BLOOD On the BARBARY COAST
By H·L·Gates

Fiends *in* Red Satin

THE SHUDDER PULPS

Grand Guignol was a notorious form of drama that originated in France at the turn of the 20th century. It gave Henry Steeger the idea for probably the most controversial of all the lines of pulp magazines.

OPPOSITE

Star Detective *often carried artwork by J.W. Scott on the cover. (See page 150)*

RIGHT

It was a Grand Guignol presentation like this one that gave Henry Steeger his idea for the weird menace pulps.

rand Guignol was popularly known as 'The Theater of Fear and Terror' and turned morbid fascination with the unpleasant into an art form. It transgressed theatrical conventions and outraged the feelings and sensibilities of audiences with just about every form of horror playwrights could devise and actors could perform without actually killing themselves. It portrayed innocent victims – often female – who were subjected to unbridled lust, torture, insanity, mutilation, and sometimes, mercifully, death. Its heyday was in the 20s and 30s when versions of some of its most famous plays – *Orgy in the Lighthouse, The Coffin of Flesh, Castle of Slow Death, The Merchant of Corpses,* and one of the

Unfortunate female victims now fell into the clutches of fiendish criminals, devilish cultists, and mad doctors and scientists.

most grisly of all, *Crucified; or, The Night of the Twelfth of May* – were performed to packed houses in Paris and several other European capitals, while some even crossed the Atlantic to the U.S. Grand Guignol has been accused of being the inspiration for the Hollywood horror pictures of the 30s and today's 'splatter movies.' Herschell Lewis, the director of *Blood Feast* and other classics of cinematic gore, wrote in 1988:

'The Grand Guignol was the progenitor of all the blood-spilling, eye-gorging, limb-hacking blood-lust boiling just under the surface of apparently civilized human beings...a marvellous mirror-image of our baser instincts.'

In an audience at one of these performances of Grand Guignol in 1933 was a young New York publisher, Henry

Steeger, and, by his own admission, what he saw gave him the idea for the 'shudder pulps.' Steeger was, in many respects, an unlikely pulp magnate. Born in New York, he had earned a degree in literature at Princeton University in 1925. After learning the art of book and magazine publishing at Dell Books, he started Popular Publications in 1930 with another bookman, Harold Goldsmith, at 205 East 42nd Street. Their first pulps were conventional enough – *Western Rangers, Gang World, Battle Aces,* and *Dime Detective,* all launched in 1931. They were followed a year later by *Dime Mystery* – intended as a companion to *Dime Detective* – but after 12 issues, Steeger sensed he needed a fresh formula if the pulp was going to survive and prosper. Years later, he explained:

'My inspiration was the Grand Guignol Theater in Paris. Each night

they put on plays in which men gouged out women's eyes and people were stabbed, garotted, and hacked up. There were horror magazines around already, of course, but with nothing like that in them.'

Steeger's idea, like that of Grand Guignol itself, was an updating of the old Gothic melodramas, especially those set during the time of the Spanish Inquisition. Almost 200 years earlier, throughout Britain and Europe, theater audiences and readers with strong constitutions had relished tales of ruined castles and mysterious dungeons in which fiends vented their depraved desires on helpless victims – mostly virgins and nuns, all of whom were incredibly beautiful and impossibly naive. Supernatural elements were often introduced into these melodramas to heighten the atmosphere of menace and human terror, although all such events

were ultimately rationalized. It was Henry Steeger who introduced these ingredients – plus the grue of Grand Guignol – to the pages of *Dime Mystery Magazine* in the fall of 1933.

Until this time, each issue of *Dime Mystery* had offered readers a long, complete detective novel. Steeger's new injection of blood called for short stories in which 'weird menace' supplanted plodding detectives. Unfortunate female victims now fell into the clutches of fiendish criminals, devilish cultists, and mad doctors and scientists – sadists of every description, some deformed, others grotesque, a few barely human in appearance. They stripped, beat, tortured, injected, and even roasted their victims for the most bizarre reasons. Often the human monsters were masked or disguised to heighten the terror and, presumably, to make detection less likely. These fiends in red satin were without equal in the pulps.

The heroes who risked life and limb – literally – to rescue these fair maidens often had to suffer in machines of torture that far outdid anything imagined during the Inquisition. Occasionally, the archvillains were women, evil temptresses with no

ABOVE LEFT

This archetypal example of fiends is by Tom Lovell for 'Coming of the Faceless Killers' by Francis James, on the cover of Dime Mystery Magazine. *(March, 1938)*

ABOVE RIGHT

A critical moment is pictured by Walter M. Baumhofer for 'My Lady of Death' by James Duncan, on the cover of Dime Mystery Magazine. *(April, 1939)*

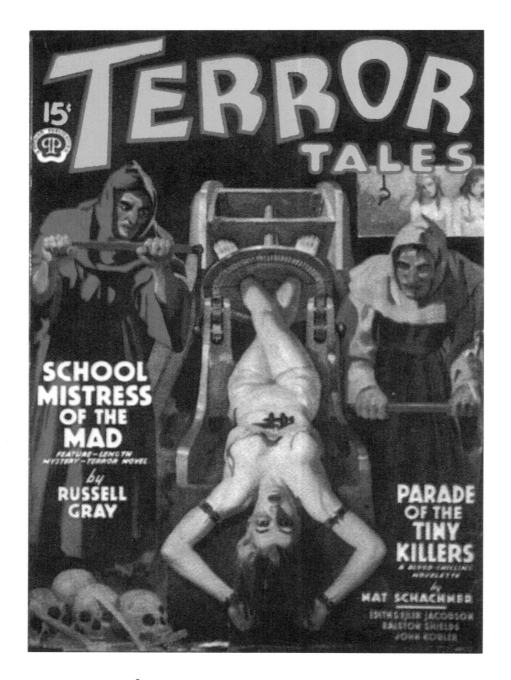

Rudolph W. Zirm dreamed up many of the incredible instruments of torture that appeared on the covers of Terror Tales. *This one illustrates 'School Mistress of the Mad' by Russell Gray. (January/February, 1939)*

scruples or, alternatively, ancient crones schooled in black magic, all adept at putting their victims through appalling terrors. Occasionally, elements of the supernatural crept into the stories, but unlike the other horror pulps – and very much in keeping with the Gothic tradition – there was always a rational explanation for them.

In the editor's column of *Dime Mystery Magazine*, 'Dark Council,' the man in charge, Rogers Terrill, spelled out the philosophy to his readers in these words:

'Horror is what a girl would feel if, from a safe distance, she watched ghouls practice diabolical rites upon a victim. Terror is what the girl would feel if, on a dark night, she heard the step of the ghoul coming toward her and knew she was marked for the next victim. Mystery is the girl wondering who done it and why.'

The revamped 10-cent package of sexual exploitation and sadism was released onto the market in October 1933 bearing the subtitle, 'The Weirdest Stories Ever Told!' It could hardly fail to find a market with its erotic cover and grisly stories provided by a group of well practiced authors including Hugh B. Cave, the British-born 'Master of the Livid Phrase' ('Dark Bondage'), and

All the old taboos went out of the window and it is no surprise that they should be remembered today as 'shudder pulps.'

the Americans, Norvell W. Page ('Music for the Lusting Dead'), Wyatt Blassingame ('Models for Madness'), and Russell Gray ('Girls for the Pain Dance'), from which this archetypal extract is taken:

'The madman paid no heed to the screams. One gloved hand twisted into the sheer fabric of the torn frock at Delia's throat. He ripped it down, baring the soft albescent contours of her breasts to his maggot-brained tampering. "Don't, please don't!" Delia strained against the leather straps that bound her wrists and ankles. "I don't want to live forever. Please –" But the fiend persisted inexorably in his purpose. Pulling the glove off his right hand, he thrust his fingers through the steel rings of the hypodermic cylinder, set his palm against the extended plunger. For a second he pawed at the trembling body of the girl. Then, viciously, he thrust the needle deep into her milk white flesh. Delia screamed again as the dread virus entered her veins...'

In the issues that followed, there was no doubting that *Dime Mystery Magazine* offered not only perversity and sadomasochism, but a genuine shudder, too – if readers could stomach all the blood, gore, and rendered female flesh being engendered by massed ranks of men they loved to loathe. All the old taboos went out of the window and it is no surprise that the group of magazines inspired by Henry Steeger's concept should be remembered today as the 'shudder pulps' – a term coined in an attack on the whole line in the *American Mercury* magazine of April 1938. The author, Bruce Henry, wrote:

'This month, as every month, 1,500,000 copies of terror magazines, known to the trade as the shudder group, will be sold throughout the nation. They contain enough illustrated sex perversion to give Krafft-Ebing the unholy jitters.'

The cover artist who became most associated with *Dime Mystery* was Tom Lovell, whose ingenuity at picturing the bizarre instruments of torture dreamed up in the pulp writers' imaginations was nothing short of remarkable. Later, his work would become familiar to the general public when he designed the logo for the Continental Insurance Company, which pictured a band of pioneers. The interior artwork was

RIGHT

Amos Sewell was a regular contributor to Terror Tales *with illustrations for tales like 'Thirst of the Ancients' by Nat Schachner. (May, 1935)*

mostly provided by the prolific Amos Sewell, whom Popular also used when it followed up the success of *Dime Mystery* with two more variations on the same theme, *Terror Tales* and *Horror Stories*.

Popular Publications' second shudder pulp, *Terror Tales*, appeared in September 1934, costing 5 cents more and claiming rather innocuously to be 'The Magazine of Eerie Fiction.' The menacing artwork by Rudolph W. Zirm indicated that what was inside might be rather strong meat – as did another editorial by Rogers Terrill:

'Did you ever as a child watch, fascinated by fear, as the shadows in your night-darkened room took on shape and form and furtive, bloodcurdling motion? Have you ever choked back a scream of blind, unreasoning terror at the sudden sharp crunch of a footfall behind you on some deserted walk? If you've undergone either of these experiences, you'll remember the quickened beating of your heart, the swifter, tingling flow of blood through your veins.

'But today, in a generation protected and coddled by the artificial safeguards of civilization, the average citizen finds scant play for those tonic bodily reflexes which are so largely caused by primitive fear. Thrills, we believe, fill an important, necessary function in any normal, healthy human life. It is the hope and aim of this magazine to counteract to some extent vicariously but none the less poignantly the regrettable lack of this age-old stimulus in present-day life...'

And that is precisely what *Terror Tales* did – probably even more unsparingly than Terrill might have suggested, thanks to the already gore-honed talents of Hugh B. Cave and Norvell W. Page, plus Ray Cummings with 'The House of Doomed Brides,' Arthur Leo Zagat describing the 'Riverfront Horror,' and Nat Schachner's 'Thirst of the Ancients,' about which the blurb enthused:

'A strange girl it was whom John Carson married – one moment pure and wholesome, the next a demon of greedy passion. Yet not till he had followed her to the home of her ancestors, till he had seen the withered, horrible ancient making ready for his feast, did John Carson guess the fearful truth.'

Inside the magazine the gritty line work of Amos Sewell was augmented by several other versatile artists, including David Berger and Paul Orban. Legend

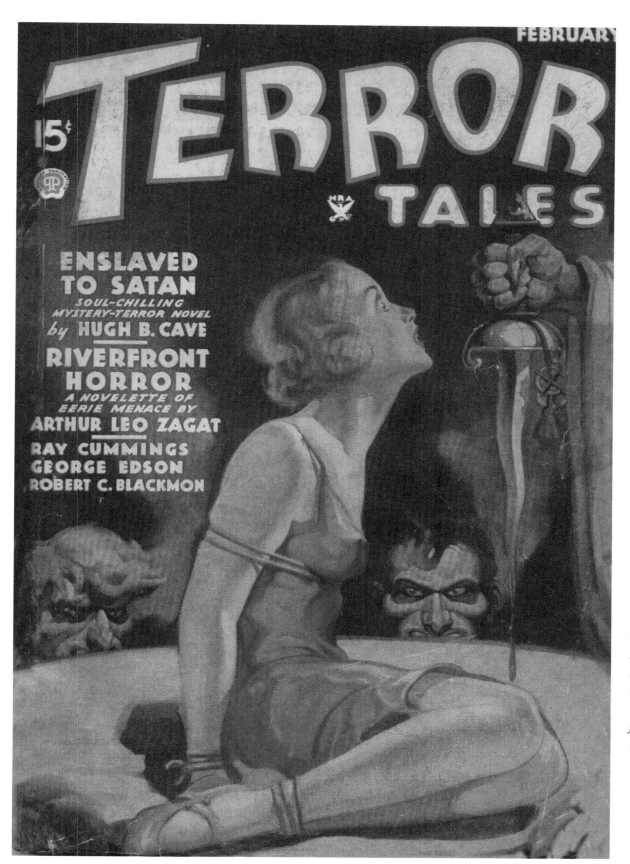

LEFT
This more traditional cover by Rudolph W. Zirm illustrates Hugh B. Cave's terror feast 'Enslaved To Satan' for Terror Tales. *(February, 1935)*

'...there she was, just as I knew she would be. Her body cold and dead and already smelling of decay.'

has it that these artists rarely saw the tales they were illustrating. They were briefed over the telephone by Rogers Terrill – who knew exactly what he wanted – and the men drew as he asked. This doubtless explains why some of the pictures in *Terror Tales* and the other Popular pulps are hard to link to the stories that they are supposed to be illustrating! Probably nowhere was this more evident than in the regular section 'The Black Chapel,' which was ostensibly a history of man's inhumanity to ˙man (and woman) ranging from the witchcraft covens of the Middle Ages to the black magicians of the 20th century.

ABOVE

This illustration was for 'Chamber of Horrors,' one of the most popular monthly features in Horror Stories.

In January 1935, the pair of Popular shudder pulps became a trio with the debut of *Horror Stories* – with its shout-line, 'Stories That Thrill and Chill.' This meant still more assignments for the company's circle of writers and the first appearance of the cover artwork of John Newton Howett, who was already familiar to some readers from his illustrations on the covers of the *Operator 5* and *The Spider* pulps. His hallmark became beautiful women whose lipstick and mascara was never smudged no matter what appalling situation they found themselves in. Inside *Horror Stories*, Amos Sewell and Richard Carlson could always be relied upon to provide suitably chilling pictures of cowled or scowling fiends up to their terrible machinations. The magazine's regular editorial column was known as the 'Chamber of Horrors,' and could be relied upon for remarkably well-informed articles on secret rituals and evil practices throughout the ages.

Apart from the regular contributors, there were several other writers who produced stories under pen-names for *Horror Stories*. Most have proved impossible to identify, with the exception of one of the most popular authors in the magazine, Donald Dale. And when the hand behind this pen was revealed, readers were in for a real shock. Dale's reputation had been built on gruesome purple prose like this in 'Tapestry of Terror:'

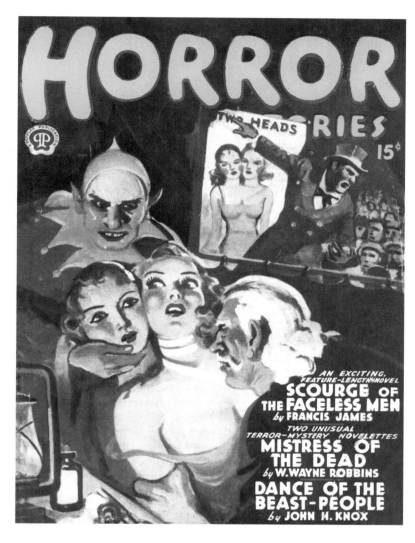

'By midnight, three shadowy figures – I and the two most desperate guet-a-pens from the lees of the slums' mixed breeds – were flitting silently back through the trees of the beautiful de Guiche burial glen. They carried spades. There was something I had to see. I had told the cut-throats about the bracelet and rings buried on the slender fingers and wrists of Madame de Guiche. And there she was, just as I knew she would be. Her body cold and dead and already smelling of decay. And that one drop of dried blood on her bosom was the only hint of the reason why that body was not lying peacefully, but was twisted and

drawn, as if in unbearable agony, and the fingers clenched so tightly that they had to be whacked off with a dirk to release the rings.

'Ecstasy filled me. Alone in the grave, without his comfort, she had suffered! While my two ghouls refilled the grave, I danced around and around it, my body light with joy and my brain drunk as with new wine. Yet, when they had gone with their loot, heaviness began again to settle upon me. I was not yet avenged on this woman who had taken the man I loved. She had not yet fully paid for those years of anguish she had given me. There must be more...'

LEFT

John Newton Howett was a regular cover artist for Horror Stories, *with work like this for 'Death Calls From The Madhouse' by Hugh B. Cave. (September, 1935)*

RIGHT

Freaks of varying kinds were a favorite subject for John Newton Howett. This illustrates the story 'Scourge of the Faceless Men' by Francis James from Horror Stories. *(December, 1938)*

ABOVE

Sinister Stories *was
another of the
shudder pulps
inspired by Grand
Guignol, as this
cover makes clear.
The artist is
unknown. (May,
1940)*

If the sex of the narrator was a giveaway, no one spotted the fact at the time. Donald Dale was actually a woman, Mary Dale Buckner, who had disguised her gender in order to break into the notoriously male-orientated field of the shudder pulps. In fact, although it had been women like Anne Radcliffe, with her *Mysteries of Udolpho*, first published in 1794, and Mary Shelley with *Frankenstein*, published in 1818, who had pioneered the Gothic genre more than a century earlier, Mary Buckner was to prove one of the very few female writers to achieve success in this latest manifestation of the old tradition.

It was in 1938 that Henry Steeger unobtrusively set up another publishing company, Fictioneers Inc., based in Chicago at 2242 Grove Street, as a kind of cut-price Popular Publications. A local journalist with the unlikely sounding name of Costa Carousso was hired to edit *Sinister Stories* and *Startling Mystery*, which Steeger decided should pay lower rates for fiction than was customary in New York and reuse a lot of the artwork from *Horror Stories* and *Terror Tales*. Out

again came the fiends in red satin and the drooling grotesques that John Newton Howett had painted earlier, while inside, a variety of black and white drawings were matched to stories with which, even the most cursory reading quickly proved, they had no connection!

As to the stories themselves, Carousso sang out the company line in an editorial in the first issue of *Sinister Stories* dated February 1940:

'In the pages of this magazine we guarantee you sense-shocking horror of the type which has until now [sic] been reserved for the patron of the Grand Guignol in Paris!'

Despite the low rates being paid, both *Sinister Stories* and *Startling Mystery* managed to secure stories by popular writers like Hugh Cave ('School Mistress for the Mad'), Wayne Rogers ('Flesh For The Devil's Piper'), Russell Gray ('Song of Evil Love'), and Donald Graham ('New Brides for the Dying'), who became a star of the three 'Red Circle' pulps to which I shall be referring shortly. Perhaps predictably, this cheapskate method for once did not work for Henry Steeger, and neither pulp lasted more than a year.

Turning the clock back, the first publisher to copy Steeger was Ned Pines who, as we have seen, built his pulp

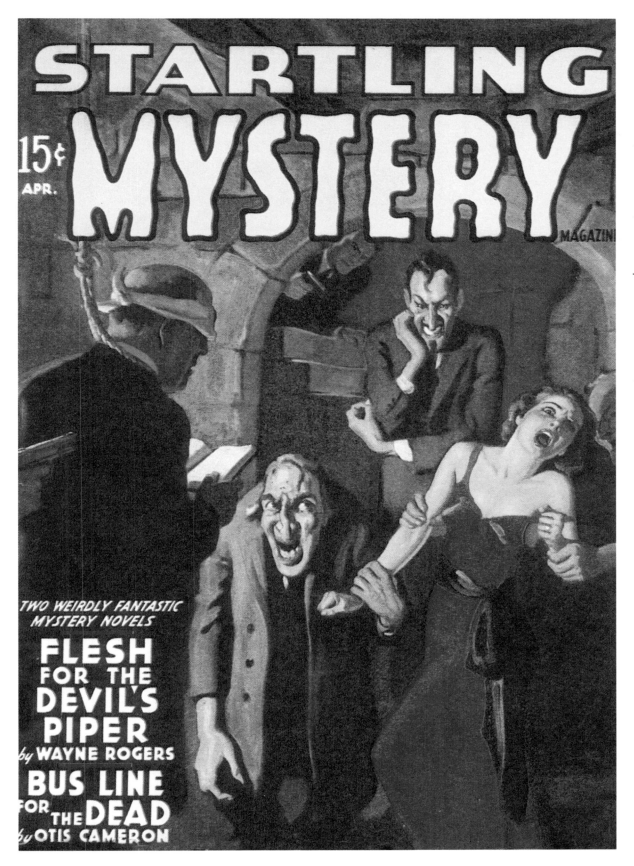

empire utilizing the word 'thrilling' as a catchall sales gimmick. He and his right-hand man, Leo Margulies, sensed the money to be made from shudder pulps and repeated Steeger's trick by revamping one of their existing titles *Thrilling Detectives* and launching a companion, *Thrilling Mystery*. Both were aimed at catering to the public taste for sex and sadism, and Margulies issued a formula to his writers that they were asked to adhere to:

'Take one or more human beings who are likeable and understandable.

Have him or them terrifically menaced by some eerie force. Be sure that a great personal fear is engendered, that life, limb and love are at stake and that the menace is someone unknown to the hero, but that it is someone in the story against whom suspicion is not at first directed.'

This said, however, the menu soon proved to be a similar dark brew of perverted criminals and deranged experimenters. Both magazines ran readers' columns, 'Headquarters' in Thrilling Detective and 'Horror-Scopes' in its companion, to which Margulies contributed himself as Harvey Burns. Among the authors who wrote for both were the great wordsmiths Arthur J. Burks ('My Companion Death'), Ray Cummings ('The Dead Who Walk'), and Joseph J. Millard, whose story 'The Corpse Marathon' contained all the basic ingredients of the classic shudder pulp story: a weird villain, a pair of lovers trapped in a subterranean cellar, and sado-sexualism awaiting them both in the shadows:

'We were in hell – but we were not dead – for this was a man-made hell! I told myself that and I fought to believe it, fought against the evidence of my own senses. How could a fleshless skeleton walk and talk? How could any

ABOVE LEFT
Nightmare meets Beauty in this Rudolph Belarski illustration for 'Mark of Death' by George A. McDonald on the cover of Thrilling Detective. *(September, 1935)*

LEFT

There is no signature on this illustration for
D. L. James's story 'The Maker of Immortality'
from Thrilling Mystery. *(June, 1940)*

human mind conceive and carry out such a scheme of horror as this? I forced myself to forget those questions, to concentrate on the one tangible thing in a nightmare of hell – the determination to somehow outwit that skeleton, man or devil, and save Fran Foster.

'I jerked my head around toward the clatter of brittle laughter and saw the skeleton standing behind us. In one fleshless hand he grasped a scourge whose multiple lashes were each tipped with a sharp-edged gold coin. As I turned, the scourge whistled through the air and liquid fire seared my back. "Welcome to hell!" the dead voice rasped and swung again at Fran Foster. "Welcome to the corpse marathon. This is your marathon. Get up and dance! You wanted Florence to dance, Craig. Well, there she lies, waiting to dance with you. Get up and dance, damn you!"'

Scenes such as this, featuring other improbable villains with green skin or fleshless faces, monstrous limbs or deformed bodies, were splashed across cover after cover of the Thrilling pulps by artists including Rudolph Belarski, who sometimes doubled up with interior artwork, along with Monroe Eisenberg, Leo Morey, Alex Schomberg, and Wynne W. Davies. Not long ago, Leo Margulies admitted that, when he did not have a

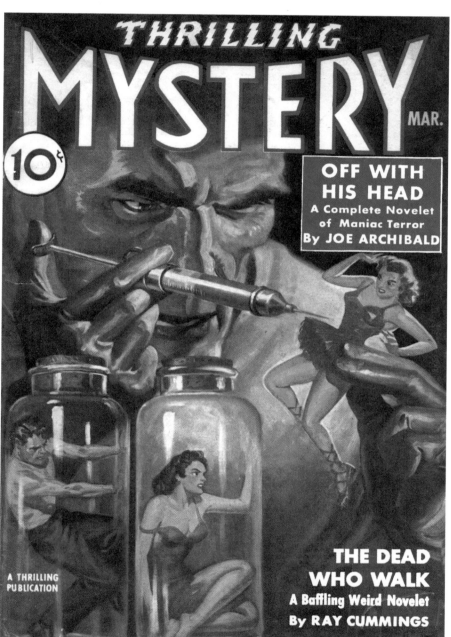

ABOVE

Thrilling Mystery, *the companion pulp to* Thrilling Detective, *featured artwork by Rudolph Belarski. This example was done for 'Off With His Head' by Joe Archibald. (March, 1940)*

'She wore black velvet and it had a sheen which set off her body with the glitter of a serpent's scales.'

suitable story for the cover, he would select a piece of artwork that had been sent in on spec by an artist desperate for work, and get one of his writers to create a story around it. These tales tended to be short and were almost invariably published under a house by-line.

Henry Steeger's publications and the Thrilling series dominated the shudder pulp market, but several other publishers were not slow in bringing out similar magazines. *New Mystery Adventures* was the first of these, the first issue appearing in March 1935. It was the handiwork of two brothers, Stanley and Whiteley Hubbard, who set themselves up as Pierre Publications at an address on West 42nd Street. Their idea was to broaden the appeal of 'weird menace' by featuring all types of stories including horror, mystery, western, historical, and high adventure. The only proviso was the old one – there had to be plenty of sex and lashings of perversion in the tales. The first editor

of *New Mystery Adventures* was a woman, Miss A. R. Roberts, but only her initials appeared on the masthead. Her tenure cannot have been a great success because the following year she was replaced by another member of the family, H. D. Hubbard.

A sample of story titles from the early issues of the magazine will give an idea of its diversity: 'The Blond Marquesan' by Wayne Rogers ('Search for a blond-haired girl reveals plans for the destruction of the entire white race – by gas!'), 'Horror Over Honolulu' by Steve Fisher ('Red-bearded Mark Turner takes a personal interest in a terror case when it threatens the happiness of an innocent, auburn-haired girl!'), and 'Rescued by Satan' by Richard Sale, which featured an evil temptress of the type found in quite a few pulp yarns at the time. She ruled a hell-ship and enforced her will on crew and victims alike with the aid of a massive tiger:

'From my perch I watched the whole horror. Kasha came first, his sinewy tail straight out behind him. He walked right up to the prow and turned. Then came Valimy. She was stunning in the moonlight. She wore black velvet and it had a sheen which set off her body with the glitter of a serpent's scales. She pointed her finger at the tiger and snapped, "Down Kasha, and be still."

'The tiger went down, half-crouched, and lay perfectly immobile. Her command of the beast was paradoxical. She went up to him with movements as graceful and silent as his own. She seemed to crouch herself – as though she, too, were a cat – and her eyes blazed a furious green in the darkness which sent shudders down my back.'

New Mystery Magazine published a number of serial stories featuring a futuristic explorer, Zenith Rand, 'Conqueror of Space and Time' by

Is this mad scientist allowing his victim a little modesty? Tom Blame's curious illustration was created for the cover of New Mystery Adventures. (December, 1935)

Richard Tooker, and stories by Wayne Roger featuring 'The Domino Lady,' an alluring amazon described as 'Ruthless and calculating, feminine and lovely, she is like Robin Hood and sets out to right the many wrongs that have been done.'

The covers of *New Mystery Adventure* were primarily the work of spite of its innocuous title, was just another haven of perversion, sadism, and sexuality. Goodman had founded Manvis Publications in 1932, issuing a number of western titles, all of which were distinguished by a red, bullet-shaped symbol bearing the words, 'A Red Circle Magazine.' This motif continued when he launched *Detective*

... *Detective Short Stories*, which, in spite of its innocuous title, was just another haven of perversion, sadism, and sexuality.

Tom Blame, who managed to make his ladies sexy and terrified without exposing quite the same acres of nudity favored by his contemporaries. Inside, much of the rather inferior artwork was unsigned, although two artists, Laurence Spinelli and Joe Chambers, did demonstrate a nice touch with exotic, native girls.

Martin Goodman is another publisher who briefly challenged the dominance of Steeger and Pines in the shudder pulps line with his 'Red Circle' pulps *Mystery Tales, Uncanny Tales,* and *Detective Short Stories*, which, in

Short Stories in November 1937, which claimed on the cover, '12 Stories for Ten Cents' and was obviously intending to outdo the existing dime pulps, which usually carried just 10 stories.

The publisher apparently made no secret of his feeling that readers of pulps were 'not interested in quality' and his editor, Robert Erisman, who had begun his career as an advertising copywriter, instructed potential authors quite simply to, 'Get sex into the story from the first paragraph.' The writers he published in *Detective Short Stories* included Hugh B. Cave, W. T. Ballard,

OPPOSITE LEFT
The title of Detective Short Stories *belied the contents – even if the artwork by J. W. Scott did not. (November, 1937)*

OPPOSITE RIGHT
The Zenith Rand adventure series was a popular feature in Mystery Adventure Magazine. *This cover was by Norman Saunders. (October, 1936)*

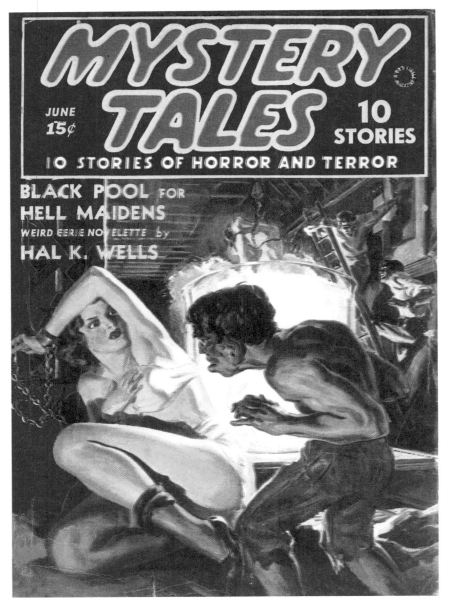

and Roger Torrey, who all piled more sex and violence into their hardboiled yarns of cops and criminals than previously. Readers were left in no doubt about the contents of the magazine because of the captive girls and malevolent fiends illustrated on the covers, a number of which were painted by Joe Simon and Jack Kirby, who would later become famous as the creators of the comic strip superhero, Captain America.

In 1938, Goodman capitalized on his success by issuing two more titles, *Mystery Tales* and *Uncanny Tales*, both of which were in-your-face packets of violence and lasciviousness. Norman Saunders once again lured readers with his brilliantly colored cover pictures of terrified beauties and the madman who wished them nothing but ill, while inside, the stories, such as 'Black Pool For Hell Maidens,' 'Pawn of Hideous Desire,' and 'I, Satan, Take Thee, Sin Child,' were credited to a variety of house names including Douglas Giles, Alan Blake, Taylor Ward, and Paul Howard. Erotic little epics by Donald Dale, a.k.a. Mary Dale Buckner, such as '...And The Blood of A Maiden,' were also to be found. One writer of this type of 'sex-sadism' fiction was Donald Graham, who became notorious as a result of his contributions to the two pulps. Stories such as 'Scourge of the

ABOVE

Another of Norman Saunders' grotesques is at work in the 'Black Pool of the Hell Maidens' by Hal K. Wells in Mystery Tales. *(June, 1938)*

LEFT

Steve Fisher's grisly story 'Return From Hell' was illustrated with remarkable restraint by Kirchner for Mystery Tales. *(May, 1939)*

Readers were left in no doubt about the contents because of the captive girls and malevolent fiends illustrated on the covers.

Corpse Clan,' 'Mates For Hell's Half-World Minions,' and 'Yield, Lovely Maidens, to the Blood Master' made him a favorite with readers, as the correspondence columns of both bear witness, month after month. In the eyes of his fans, few other writers in the shudder pulps could match Graham when it came to describing sadistic freaks, bacchanalian orgies, and women made helpless by bondage, drugs, or debauchery.

However, too much of a bad thing ultimately leads to only one thing, and, as the 30s drew to a close, it was becoming evident that the public appetite for sex and sadism was dwindling. Three further examples of the shudder pulps will therefore suffice for this particular aspect of pulp history: *Star Detective*, *Detective Yarns*, and *Eerie Mysteries*.

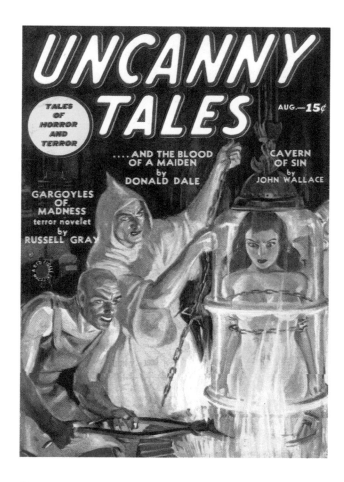

ABOVE

Norman Saunders' brush was at work here for Donald Dale's story '.... And The Blood Of A Maiden,' featured in Uncanny Tales. *(August, 1939)*

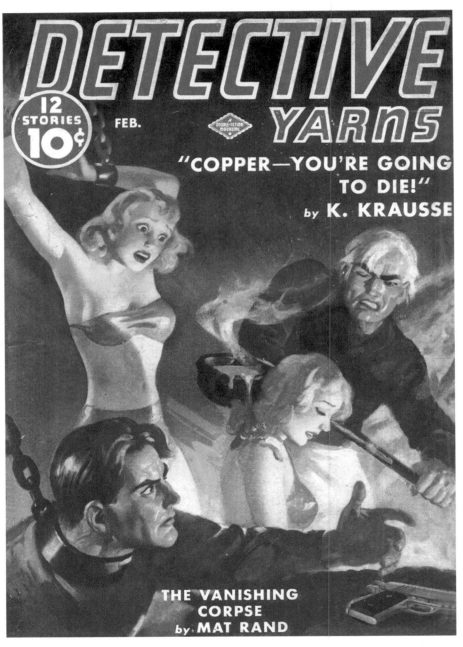

ABOVE LEFT

One of J. W. Scott's best covers for Star Detective *illustrates 'Blood on the Barbary Coast' by H. L. Gates. (May, 1935)*

ABOVE

William Reusswig painted numerous covers for the pulps, including this archetypal scene for Detective Yarns. *Curiously, it does not occur in any story in the magazine! (February, 1939)*

'A ghastly, bloody thing that was a man staggered out of San Francisco tulle fog to start a reign of terror that reached even to the city's millionaires.'

Star Detective and *Detective Yarns* fell into the same category as *Detective Short Stories*. They covered a multitude of sins although their covers were rather less gruesome than those of *Detective Short Stories*, and their female victims were more decently clothed. *Star Detective* was published by the Western Fiction Publishing Co. at 11 West 42nd Street, under the editorship of James Randall, a man who preferred longer stories. In fact, he often filled as much as two-thirds of the magazine with the likes of 'Blood on the Barbary Coast' by H. L. Gates, trailing it with the lines, 'A ghastly, bloody thing that was a man staggered out of San Francisco tulle fog to start a reign of terror that reached even to the city's millionaires.' The other contributors included Conrad Gerson and Edward Doherty, who wrote tales of ruthless mobsters, violent killers, and Oriental fiends all nursing grievances against beautiful girls. The magazine rather skimped on the interior art by L. J. Bjornland, but the covers by J. W. Scott were never less than excellent.

Detective Yarns was one of the 'Double-Action Magazines,' a line of pulps founded in 1934 by Louis Silberkleit of the Winford Company based at 60 Hudson Street in New York. Silberkleit had begun his career working for Hugo Gernsback, the 'founding father' of the science fiction pulps, and he had evidently learned a great deal from his boss's canny business sense about how to succeed in pulp publishing. In time, the Double Action Magazine group would have more than two dozen titles, which were operated entirely on how well they sold on the newsstands and bookstalls. All the Winford pulps carried the line, 'A Dozen Stories For A Dime.'

The editor of *Detective Yarns* was listed as Cliff Campbell, but this was actually a pseudonym for Abner Sundell, the editor of several of the company's other mainstream titles. Perhaps he was not overly keen on being associated with blood-soaked little gems of purple prose like 'Copper – You're Going To Die!' by K. Krausse, 'Hot Ice

'Shrieking coffins with grisly cargoes plunge the peaceful campus into an apoplexy of terror.'

Is No Good In Hell' by Dale De V. Kier, and 'Hot Squat Fade Out' by Dugal MacDougal, all of which may well have been by one and the same wordsmith. The major cover artist was William Reusswig, while the interior artwork was usually by Jack Gehti, whose scenes of sexual assault and torture were already beginning to look rather passé.

Indeed, when *Eerie Mysteries* was issued in October 1938 by A. A. Wyn's Ace Fiction Group, it was obvious that the shudder pulps were fading fast. Boasting of containing, '10 Complete Horror-Thrillers,' the story titles of *Eerie Mysteries* were strong but less sexually suggestive than previously. Take, for example, 'When It Rained Corpses' by Ralph Powers ('Shrieking coffins with grisly cargoes plunge the peaceful campus into an apoplexy of terror'), 'The Robot's Revenge' by Dennis Storm ('Manhattan is chilled by the ghastly spectacle of a man without a brain'), and 'Skull and Double-Cross Bones' by Eric Lennon ('The beautiful woman martyr had a grinning skull for a head').

Descriptions of beautiful females being molested and tortured were notably fewer, while the uncredited cover art of *Eerie Mysteries* was a throwback to more prosaic days. What little interior illustration there was bore every indication of being material reused from companion publications in the Ace group. In fact, a number of the pulp publishers tried to save on costs by reprinting old stories under new titles. When complaints were laid against them to the authorities by readers, Wyn, Martin Goodman, and Louis Silberkleit, as well as several others, were ordered by the Federal Trade Commission to state clearly when a story was appearing in print for a second time. If they did not, they risked being shut down.

It all amounted to a tawdry end for Henry Steeger's brainwave. But then Steeger had always been a hardheaded businessman and never expected to win any awards for promoting literature. He gained the satisfaction – and financial rewards – of being a major player in the pulp market for almost a decade. He commented some years later:

'By the start of the 40s, with the nation on the verge of war, there was a kind of moral backlash. We had the permissiveness and thrilling-seeking in the 30s, but that changed. It was the social pressures that killed off the pulps.'

OPPOSITE

This cover for an issue of Eerie Mysteries, *one of the last of the shudder pulps, is by Norman Saunders. (November, 1938)*

10 COMPLETE HORROR-THRILLERS
EERIE
MYSTERIES
NOVEMBER
15¢
WHEN IT
AINED CORPSES
Novelette of Weird Doom
RALPH POWERS
SONG OF
SPECTRE
RONALD
LAGG

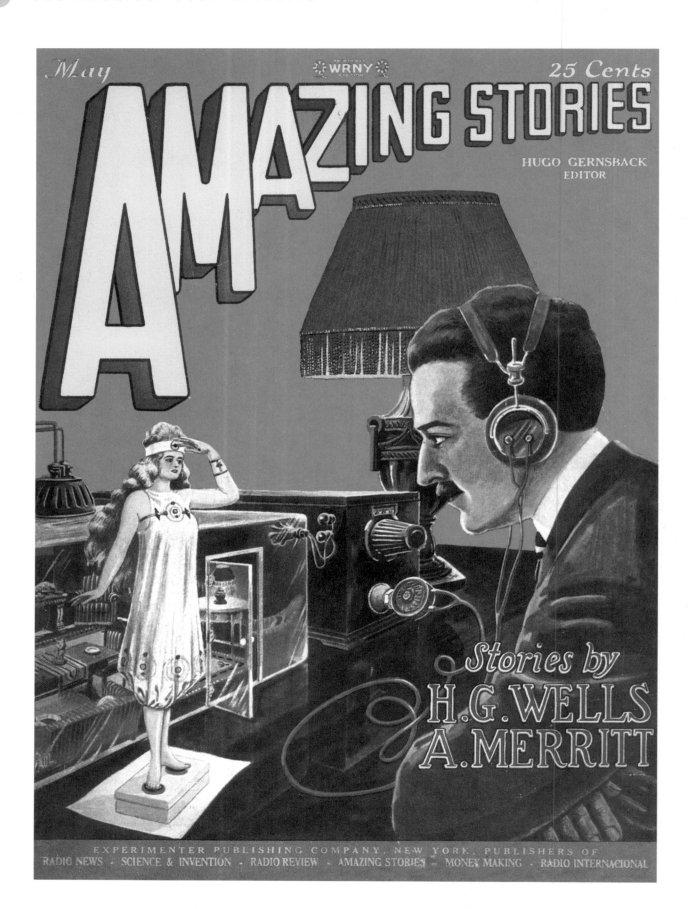

Knobheads *and* Other B.E.M.s

THE SCI-FI PULPS

On April 5, 1926, a new publication called *Amazing Stories* hit the newsstands of the United States. The cover showing an ice-covered world with Saturn in the background indicated the type of story inside, which was soon to become known as science fiction.

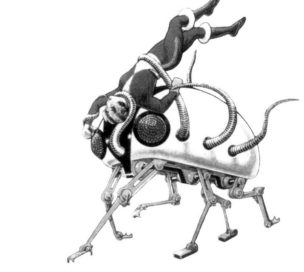

RIGHT

This maiden in distress
appeared on the cover of
Wonder Stories. *(March, 1933)*
(See page 159)

OPPOSITE

Frank Paul, 'The Father of
Modern Sci-fi Illustration,'
illustrated this cover of
Amazing Stories. *(May, 1927)*

The impression given by the cover illustration of the first issue of *Amazing Stories* was confirmed by four lines of lettering in bold type: 'Stories by H. G. Wells, Jules Verne, and Edgar Allen [sic] Poe.' In smaller letters below the title ran the legend, 'Hugo Gernsback, Editor' and at the very bottom were the words 'Experimenter Publishing Company, New York.' The arrival of this, the first sci-fi magazine in the world, amounted to a remarkable achievement of vision and determination by the editor and it was to have the most far-reaching impact on the

'There is the usual fiction magazine and the sex-appeal magazine, the adventure type and so on, but a magazine of "Scientification" is a pioneer in its field in America.'

entire genre. On the title page of the new magazine, beneath a sub-heading that read 'The Magazine of Scientification,' was an editorial by Gernsback that almost leapt off the page with its enthusiasm:

'Amazing Stories is a new kind of fiction magazine! It is entirely new – entirely different – something that has never been done before in this country. Therefore Amazing Stories deserves your attention and interest. There is the usual fiction magazine and the sex-appeal magazine, the adventure type and so on, but a magazine of "Scientification" is a pioneer in its field in America. By "Scientification" I mean the Jules Verne, H. G. Wells, and Edgar Allan Poe type of story – a charming romance intermingled with scientific fact and prophetic vision. Edgar Allan Poe may well be called the father of "Scientification." It was he who really originated the romance, cleverly weaving into and around the story, a scientific thread. Jules Verne with his amazing romances, also interwoven with a scientific thread, came next. A little later came H. G. Wells whose scientification stories, like those of his forerunners, have become famous and immortal. Many great science fiction stories destined to be of an historical interest are still being written, and Amazing Stories will be the medium through which such stories will come to you. Posterity will point to them as having blazed a new trail, not only in literature and fiction, but in progress as well.'

Brave new words. Observing that the U.S. was now living in a time of increasing scientific discovery, Gernsback stated that 'elaborate plans have been laid sparing neither time nor money' to produce *Amazing Stories*, which would be exclusively devoted to publishing this new kind of fiction. He added, 'The formula in all cases is that the story must be frankly amazing; second, it must contain a scientific background; third, it must possess originality.' However – and perhaps taking the easy option – the editor almost filled the first issue with stories by his mentors: Poe's 'The Facts in the Case of M. Valdemar,' Verne's 'Off on a Comet,' and H. G. Wells's 'The New Accelerator.' In the following months, too, there would rarely be an issue that did not contain a reprint from one or more of this trio. The pulp was, though, an undeniable success, and has been published in one format or another ever since.

Today, Hugo Gernsback is acknowledged as the 'father' of the sci-fi magazine. He was born in Luxembourg, the son of a wealthy wine merchant, and became fascinated with science through reading the stories of Poe, Verne, and Wells. Gernsback was also something of an inventor, and during his years at the Ecole Industrielle in Luxembourg, he devised plans for improvements in the telephone and several other forms of electrical communications that were just then coming into use. However, unable to gain any commercial interest in these ideas, he emigrated to the land of opportunity, the United States, in 1904. There, after unsuccessful attempts to design a mass-produced battery and market home radio sets, Gernsback tried publishing instead and, in 1908, founded the first radio magazine,

RIGHT
Frank Paul's work appeared throughout the pages of Amazing Stories *illustrating tales such as 'The Princess of Aphur' by David H. Keller. (October, 1928)*

Modern Electrics. He wrote a prophetic serial story for the periodical, 'Ralph 124C 41+,' and, bouyed by its success, launched a second publication, *Electrical Experimenter*, in 1915. Once again he produced a fictional series, 'Baron Munchausen's New Scientific Adventures,' in which the eccentric teller of tall stories traveled to Mars. Gernsback also encouraged other writers to contribute stories of the same kind to the magazine and the response gave him the idea, in 1926, of producing a pulp devoted solely to 'Scientification.' Earlier publications like Munsey's *Argosy* and *Cavalier* had occasionally run this type of story, but *Amazing Stories* would be the first devoted to 'flights of imagination.'

After the initial flurry of reprints by the classic sci-fi authors, Gernsback launched the careers of a number of important writers including Abraham Merritt, Murray Leinster, David H. Keller, and Jack Williamson. He also published the first space opera, *Buck Rogers in the 25th Century* by Philip Francis Nowlan, the hero of which would later become a star of comics, movies, and also television. Gernsback launched the career of E. E. 'Doc' Smith, with his series about the hero-inventor

Richard Seaton battling the villainous, Marc 'Blackie' DuQuesne. The series commenced in 1928 with *The Skylark of Space*. The success of *Amazing Stories* prompted Gernsback to publish an *Amazing Stories Annual* in 1927, which scored another first by printing Edgar Rice Burroughs's 'The Master Mind of Mars.' The annual's success in turn generated *Amazing Stories Quarterly*, which ran for 22 issues from 1928 to 1934 and again introduced some important new writers, namely John W. Campbell Jr., Stanton A. Coblentz, and A. Hyatt Verrill.

From the very first issue of *Amazing Stories* until 1929, when the threat of being made bankrupt forced Gernsback to relinquish control, all the covers and interior artwork were done by Frank

An innovation for the magazine was its sponsorship of the 'Science Fiction League,' which was to play a major role in the development of sci-fi fandom in the States.

Rudolph Paul, a fellow ex-European whom the editor had found working on a rural newspaper. Born in Austria, Paul was educated in Vienna and Paris, and came to New York to complete his training as an architect. Unable to find employment in this field, however, he settled for newspaper hackwork. Gernsback discovered him and offered him employment on *Amazing Stories*. Although Paul's style was a curious mixture of the primitive and the technological – and his human figures, especially women in moments of danger, rather coy and wooden – his work deservedly earned him the sobriquet, 'The Father of Modern science fiction Illustration.'

After parting company from *Amazing Stories* in 1929, Gernsback set up a new company, Stellar Publishing Corporation, at 96 Park Place, New York, and a little while later released three new sci-fi magazines. Two of these, *Air Wonder Stories* and *Science Wonder Stories*, lasted less than a year before being amalgamated as *Wonder Stories*, while the third, *Scientific Detective Monthly*, managed just 10 monthly issues, although it did represent another 'first' in pulp history.

Air Wonder Stories was the first of the trio to appear (in July 1929). It was edited by David Lasser, who announced in his first editorial that it would publish 'solely flying stories of the future, strictly along scientific-mechanical-technical lines.' With this in mind, he had hired an air corps major as an adviser, as well as three professors of science. However, despite contributions by established authors Edmond Hamilton, David Keller, and Jack Williamson, the magazine was merged

Frank Paul created this early
example of a maiden in distress on
the cover of the sci-fi pulp Wonder
Stories. *(March, 1933)*

with *Science Wonder Stories* the following May. *Science Wonder Stories* had first appeared in June 1929, edited by Gernsback himself, and once again he claimed that every story in it would be 'scientifically feasible.' He signed up several of the talented writers he had nurtured on *Amazing Stories*, including Keller, Williamson, and Gallun, but only 12 issues reached the newsstands before the amalgamation.

Wonder Stories fared rather better than its parents. Gernsback worked in tandem with David Lasser on the text, while Frank Paul drew all the covers and a great many of the interior illustrations. An innovation for the magazine was its sponsorship of the 'Science Fiction League,' which was to play a major role in the development of sci-fi fandom in the States. It also first published some ground-breaking stories

'The Electrical Man' wore electrically powered clothes that repelled anything fired at him and could stun any villain foolish enough to try to attack him.

by Clark Ashton Smith and Britain's John Wyndham (then known by his real name of John Beynon Harris). In the spring of 1936, the pulp was sold to Ned Pines. It reappeared in August as *Thrilling Wonder Stories* and began a new era of success.

Scientific Detective Monthly was Gernsback's pioneering attempt to link science and the solving of crime, and he proudly labeled himself on the cover as 'Editorial Chief.' The first issue appeared in January 1930, and once more the publisher lined up a number of experts to help, including two professors of criminology, Edwin J. Cooley and Henry A. Higgins, the 'Scientific Criminologist' C. P. Mason, and – most curious of all – a French deputy inspector, Lucien Fournier! As editor, Gernsback hired Arthur B. Reeve, the creator of Craig Kennedy the 'Scientific Detective,' who had made his debut way back in 1910 in the pages of *Cosmopolitan*. Kennedy was now to continue his career as the 'star attraction' in *Scientific Detective Monthly*. The dependable Edmond Hamilton and the writing partnership of Edwin Balmer and William B. MacHarg contributed stories that occasionally mixed elements of sci-fi amidst all the test tubes and murder. The pulp also introduced the very first 'superhero,' Miller Rand, 'The Electrical Man.' He wore electrically powered clothes – including hat, gloves, and socks – that repelled anything fired or shot at him and could stun any villain foolish enough to try to attack him. Created by Neil R. Jones, a New York insurance company claims investigator, Rand has been described by several sci-fi historians as a forerunner of Superman and all the other invincible crime fighters. Although Frank R. Paul was responsible for some of the interior artwork in *Scientific Detective Monthly*, the covers were the exclusive domain of a more traditional artist, John Ruger, who had previously worked for a number of the slick magazines.

Hugo Gernsback died in 1967 and, although there has been much debate about his true role in science fiction, his influence was certainly profound and his name is honored in the prestigious Science Fiction Achievement Awards known as 'Hugos.' His accomplishments in the editorial chair at *Amazing Stories* were furthered by several of his successors, notably Raymond A. Palmer and Cele Lalli. Palmer was put in charge of the pulp in 1938, when sales

OPPOSITE

This cover for Amazing Stories *by Robert Gibson Jones has an illustration for one of Richard S. Shaver's controversial stories, 'Titan's Daughter.' (September, 1948)*

ABOVE RIGHT

The first superhero, Miller Rand, 'The Electrical Man,' was drawn by John Ruger for Scientific Detective Monthly. *(May, 1930)*

He published a controversial series of allegedly 'true' fantasies about the lost continent of Lemuria and an evil race of subterraneans.

had fallen substantially, and he proceeded to boost them right back up again by negotiating with Edgar Rice Burroughs for new stories – including 'John Carter and the Giant of Mars' – and he published a controversial series of allegedly 'true' fantasies by Richard S. Shaver about the lost continent of Lemuria and an evil race of subterraneans who the author claimed were now controlling everything that happened on the surface world from mysterious disappearances to world wars. Sales rocketed, but readers were understandably divided about the theory, which became known as 'The Shaver Mystery.' The covers of the issues containing these stories were superbly illustrated by Robert Gibson Jones. Palmer's successor, Cele Lalli, was one of the few women editors in sci-fi, and she took the magazine to new heights by promoting quality writing and nurturing several talented new authors including Marion Zimmer

Bradley, Harlan Ellison, and Roger Zelazny. Between them – and in their very different ways – Palmer and Lalli ensured that the legend that Hugo Gernsback had created did not die.

The relaunching of *Wonder Stories* in August 1936, with the added suffix, Thrilling, heralded a long life for the magazine. It was to continue for more than 100 issues, appearing until 1955 either as a bi-monthly or quarterly, astutely edited throughout these years by, firstly Leo Margulies then Mort Weisinger, Sam Merwin Jr., and Alexander Samalman. The first editorial by Weisinger, in August 1936, was an echo of Gernsback's 10 years earlier:

'Here it is! *Thrilling Wonder Stories* – and under new ownership! Bound in no tradition but the high standard of quality in imaginative fiction set by Jules Verne, H. G. Wells, Lord Dunsany, and other masters [what had Poe done wrong?]. Dedicated to the exploration of unknown worlds, the prophecy of things to come. Advisedly, the word Thrilling has been added to the title of this magazine. For what can be more thrilling than man's excursion into the unknown – his never-ending quest for greater knowledge of natural forces?'

Future issues promised readers 'the greatest masterpieces by the superior

OPPOSITE

Earle Bergey, 'The Inventor of the Brass Brassiere,' illustrating a cover of Thrilling Wonder Stories, *producing an archetypal example of his work. (August, 1950)*

THRILLING WONDER STORIES

AUG.
25¢

FEATURED NOVELETS
AS YOU WERE
By HENRY KUTTNER

THE WEARIEST RIVER
By WALLACE WEST

NEW BODIES FOR OLD
By JACK VANCE

writers in the field' naming Ray Cummings, Jack Williamson, Edmond Hamilton, and Ralph Milne Farley – 'the men who are blazing the trail of science fiction's twentieth-century Hall of Fame.' *Thrilling Wonder Stories* introduced one of the first sci-fi comic strips, Zarnak, drawn by the crime story illustrator Max Plaisted, as well as some fiction series that proved very popular with readers: John W. Campbell Jr.'s 'Penton and Blake' tales, the Gerry Carlyle adventures written by Arthur K. Barnes, and Henry Kuttner's whacky yarns about 'Hollywood on the Moon.' Among regular features were 'Scientifacts – Incredible But True!' a correspondence column, 'The Reader Speaks,' conducted by Sergeant Saturn, and during the years of the Second World War, 'Wonders of War: The Role of Science in Combat on All Fronts,' which encouraged readers to 'Buy War Stamps and Bonds.' The magazine also became the official channel of news for the Science Fiction League.

Thrilling Wonder Stories scored with readers in another way, too – its art. Paul was replaced by the versatile and imaginative Earle Bergey, the 'inventor of the brass brassiere.' His training as a commercial artist, he explained some years later, made him rather less interested in the technology of space travel, which dominated the work of his

predecessors, and more in the human beings caught up in the drama of space travel. The attire of his female characters was always rudimentary, no matter what kind of environment they found themselves in, or what manner of threat was posed by menacing Bug Eyed Monsters (B.E.M.s). The merits of his covers were, as a result, a regular topic of debate in the letters column, as in this example by Bill Stoy:

'The covers by Bergey are consistently good. A lack of lurid and screaming colors with a substitution of more subtle shades and tints, realistic B.E.M.s – which, because of this quality are not offensive to the eye – has resulted in some really good works of art, neatly executed in all

respects. In short, they are oil paintings good enough to have been done by Virgil Finlay.'

Among those who handled the line artwork inside *Thrilling Wonder Stories* were Leo Morey, Paul Orban, and Tom Marchioni, who took a lead from Bergey and clothed many of his female characters in a similar range of exotic brassieres. There was also work by the aforementioned Virgil Finlay, who needed little incentive when it came to devising forms of female decolletage.

In January 1939, Popular capitalized on the success of *Thrilling Wonder* by issuing a companion pulp, *Startling Stories*. Mort Weisinger was again the editor and promised readers

STARTLING STORIES

5¢

SPRING ISSUE

A THRILLING PUBLICATION

RED SUN OF DANGER
A Captain Future Novel
By BRETT STERLING

THE ISLE OF UNREASON
A Hall of Fame Story
By EDMOND HAMILTON

'I read these magazines when I had to hide them from my mother or see them burned and I liked them.'

full-length sci-fi 'novels' – although they were actually no more than novelettes. The magazine ran for 99 issues until 1955, publishing an impressive list of authors with some of their best work, namely Manly Wade Wellman ('Giants of Eternity'), Fredric Brown ('What Mad Universe'), and Arthur C. Clarke ('Against the Fall of Night'). In the years that immediately followed the Second World War, *Startling Stories* also ran a series of adventures about Captain Future, a superhero who had his own magazine from 1940 to 1944. The stories of the captain, one Curt Newton, 'The Wizard of Science,' and his assistants, Grag, a giant metal robot, Otho, a synthetic android, and Simon Wright 'The Living Brain,' were written by Edmond Hamilton under the pseudonym Brett Sterling. The pulp also conducted a 'Hall of Fame' section in which reprints of some of the classics from the days of Hugo Gernsback were given a new airing. There were three regular columns: 'They Changed The World,' 'Thrills in Science' (written by Mort Weisinger), and a 'Review of Science Fiction Fan Magazines,' which demonstrated the increasing interest in the genre. Indeed it was becoming apparent from pages like this that it was not only men who were interested in sci-fi. Take Grace Mosher, for example, who felt compelled to write to *Startling Stories* in response to some less than chivalrous comments from a member of the opposite sex:

'May a mere woman reader of fifteen years standing say something to that big lug Rodney "Rodway" Palmer? You know he is really asking to be put in his place. I, as a silent fan of long standing, will agree with him that the old authors were good. So are those of today. My dear Rod, where would you be if it weren't for a woman? Don't belittle us. I read these magazines when I had to hide them from my mother or see them burned and I liked them. I'll admit that some of the dry scientific data went over my head, but for years I have returned again and again to the same magazine. I've made a great many others read them by lending or giving mine and have helped fandom to grow. I know how I feel and, after fifteen years, I don't feel like changing my style of reading just to please a man!'

OPPOSITE
'Red Sun of Danger' is a Captain Future adventure by Brett Sterling. It was illustrated by Earle Bergey for Startling Stories. *(Spring, 1946)*

extremely popular with those readers who preferred rampant technology to rampant sexuality. Brown, who had studied at the Chicago Art Institute and had been employed for years as the cover artist for *Scientific American*, brought a verisimilitude to his pictures that made even the most outlandish of his machines seem possible. Some of his illustrations of monsters stamping through the streets of busy cities destroying everything in their path may well have inspired the later makers of sci-fi disaster movies. The interior art was divided between Herman Vestal, Jack Binder, and Alex Schomberg, who, like several others in the field, had begun his career working for Hugo Gernsback. During a career that lasted 65 years, Schomberg became known as 'the king of the airbrush.' His light touch lent itself naturally to humor and some of the best examples of this aspect of his talent are to be found in the pages of *Startling Stories*.

During its final decade, *Startling Stories* was claimed by some experts to be the best sci-fi pulp on the market. Others felt the honor belonged to *Astounding Stories*, which was launched in January 1930 by the short-lived Clayton Magazines group, but then taken over by Street & Smith and, thanks to successive owners Conde Naste, Davis Publications, and Dell

The redoubtable Grace said she had no objections to the way women were portrayed in the sci-fi magazines and voted Earle Bergey – who was also producing a large number of the *Startling Stories* covers – as the 'best in the business.' Startling also used the artistic talents of Howard V. Brown, whose pictures of huge scientific machines dwarfing humanity were

TOP
This is one of Howard V. Brown's awesome machines that tramped across the covers of Startling Stories *during the 40s. (July, 1939)*

LEFT
An interior illustration in Thrilling Wonder Stories *by Howard V. Brown pictures a 'monster' threat from 'Battle of the Brains' by Jerry Shelton. (Spring, 1946)*

...huge scientific **machines** were extremely **popular** with those **readers** who preferred rampant **technology** to rampant **sexuality.**

ABOVE
H. W. Wesso produced this illustration of 'The Beetle Horde' by Victor Rousseau during his exceptional period as artist to Astounding Stories. (February, 1930)

TOP RIGHT
The comic style of Alex Schomberg is seen at its best in this illustration for 'The Crook in Time' by R. J. McGregor from Startling Stories. *(October, 1939)*

Magazines, survived as a magazine, albeit in digest size, to the present day. Harry Bates was the first editor, followed later by John W. Campbell Jr., Ben Bova, and Stanley Schmidt. Bates's original policy of action-adventure stories, in which science was not expected to underpin every element, the way Gernsback demanded, found an enthusiastic readership that enjoyed the rousing fare provided by Sewell Peaslee Wright, Ray Cummings, and Frank Belknap Long. Bates himself, with the help of *Astounding Stories*' assistant editor Desmond Hall, wrote a popular 'space opera' featuring Hawk Carse and his black assistant, Friday, whose mission was to rid the universe of the evil Dr. Ku Sui. The magazine carried science features by the famous German rocket scientist Willy Ley, who was by then working on space propulsion for the U.S. The covers of every issue of the magazine, while it belonged to the Clayton Group, were by the peerless Wesso.

Marvel Science Stories, which was published from 1938 to 1941 by Postal Publications of 350 Fifth Avenue, New York, was the first of the sci-fi magazines to become notorious for deliberately introducing erotic elements into its stories. The editor, Robert O. Erisman, mixed traditional sci-fi tales by Henry Kuttner and Jack Williamson with rather more raunchy stuff that he hoped would attract readers looking for more titillation than was usual in sci-fi. Stories with titles like 'World Without Sex' by Robert Wentworth and 'Lust Rides the Roller Coaster' by Ray King tell their own story. Perhaps not surprisingly, Erisman favored the talents of artist Norman Saunders, who

... two astronauts could be seen man-handling a girl wearing diaphanous robes – and nothing else – into the hold of an orbiting spaceship!

had, of course, worked for various of the weird and horror pulps. His cover for the April/May 1939 issue of a naked beauty in a curious vibratory machine lacked only a leering mad scientist to be ideally suited for his other markets.

After a decade of absence, *Marvel Science Stories* was revived in digest size in 1951, with Erisman once again in the editorial chair. This time the magazine became involved in a quite different kind of controversy, when it carried a special feature in the May issue about Scientology with L. Ron Hubbard, Lester del Ray, and Theodore Stugeon arguing the pros and cons of 'The Dianetics Question.' This very collectable issue – which contained an Arthur C. Clarke short story, 'Captain Wyxtpthll's Flying Saucer,' and 'The Thing' by Richard Matheson – also had a cover by Norman Saunders in which two astronauts could be seen man-handling a girl wearing diaphanous robes – and nothing else – into the hold of an orbiting spaceship!

With the straightforward title *Science Fiction*, there was no mistaking the intention of the new pulp from Blue Ribbon Magazines, which appeared on the newsstands in March 1939. The editor was Charles D. Hornig, who had worked on *Wonder Stories*, so it was not surprising to find that *Science Fiction* featured work by several of the writers who had been contributors to his previous publication. He added the veterans Ray Cummings, Eando Binder, and Stanton A. Coblentz. For the cover art he relied largely on the evergreen Frank R. Paul, although Peter Poulton,

who illustrated a number of the short stories, had a fine eye that was very evident on one early tale by Anne McCaffrey, 'Freedom of the Race,' about an alien experiment in pregnancy. Like Robert Erisman, Hornig often devoted space in the magazine to a cause, and several issues of *Science Fiction* trumpeted the case for the 'new world language,' Esperanto. Hornig's expansive claims were rather comic, although readers probably got a bigger chuckle from one of the most absurd titles ever to be given to a sci-fi story: 'Planet of the Knob Heads.' This was Stanton A. Coblentz's 'astounding new book-length novel' published in the December 1939 issue.

In November 1939, Blue Ribbon launched a companion pulp, *Future Fiction*, which was also edited by Hornig and provided more fiction by the same authors. The cover art, however,

was handled by Milton Luros, who displayed his virile heroines in a variety of exotic brassieres that would not have disgraced Bergey, while Peter Poulton produced the lion's share of the interior art. The independence of the two magazines did not survive long, however, for in October 1941 they were amalgamated under the clumsy title *Future Combined with Science Fiction*. The pulp also got a new editor, Robert W. Lowndes, who ensured its future by introducing a new wave of writers, notably C. M. Kornbluth and Margaret St. Clair. The readers' letters section 'Down To Earth' prompted mail that went beyond the normal mixture of praise and complaints. Instead, it generated quite technical arguments about the science behind the stories, which Lowndes encouraged his authors to respond to. Under his diligent stewardship, the magazine – which

became *Future Fantasy and Science Fiction* in October 1942 and ultimately *Future Science Fiction* – continued after the War in digest size until it finally ceased publication in 1960.

Planet Stories, which Fiction House Magazines of New York put out in that winter of discontent of 1939, when Europe had just been plunged into war, has become famous as the 'archetypal

ABOVE LEFT

Peter Poulton illustrated 'Freedom of the Race' by Anne McCaffrey for Science Fiction. *(May, 1939)*

ABOVE

This classic Frank Paul illustration is for Stanton Coblentz's absurdly titled 'Planet of the Knob Heads' for Science Fiction. *(December, 1939)*

...the enticing women and rugged men that [Kelly Freas] drew for the dramatic black and white spreads of *Planet Stories* were only the start...

sci-fi pulp.' According to Brian Aldiss, 'its brisk, preposterous, glossy, highly purchasable covers' came to typify the general public's perception of the sci-fi pulps, and stories such as 'Temptress of Planet Delight' by B. Curtis, 'The Pit of Nymphons' by Stanley Muller, and 'The Black Amazon of Mars' by Leigh Brackett, only confirmed such prejudice. In fact, over the years, managing editor Malcom Reiss attracted some fine talents to his pages, including Ray Bradbury, Isaac Asimov, Leigh Brackett, Paul Anderson, and Philip K. Dick, who published his very first story, 'Beyond Lies The Wub,' in *Planet Stories*. Two artists vied to produce its most garish covers: the Hungarian-born Alexander Leydenfrost, the son of an illustrator, who was an excellent black and white stylist of the grotesque, and Fred Anderson, a New York graphic artist, who brought the vivid use of

colors that he had practiced in advertising to the covers of the magazine.

Planet Stories thrived throughout the 40s, and in 1950 the magazine was instrumental in introducing to the world the remarkable talent of Frank Kelly Freas, who some critics claim to be the most popular artist in sci-fi. Be that as it may, the enticing women and rugged men that he drew for the dramatic black and white spreads of *Planet Stories* were only the start of a career that would lead to him painting covers for the digest-sized sci-fi magazines and the front page of *Mad* magazine, and ultimately designing the shoulder patch for the NASA astronauts who were on the Skylab 1 mission. Freas has deservedly won numerous awards for his illustrations, and several portfolios of his work have been published, most notable of which is *Frank Kelly Freas: The Art of Science Fiction* (1977).

RIGHT TOP

Female clothing became no more substantial when Future *combined with* Science Fiction. *No cover artist was credited for this illustration. (Winter, 1941)*

RIGHT BOTTOM

Modesty began to affect the heroines of the sci-fi magazines as demonstrated in this uncredited cover for an issue of Science Fiction Quarterly. *(February, 1952)*

ABOVE

One of Alexander Leydenfrost's impressive covers for Planet Stories *illustrates 'The Thing of Venus' by Wilbur S. Peacock. (Spring, 1942)*

In 1940, Popular Publications launched *Super Science Stories* under the banner of its subsidiary company, Fictioneers Inc. The pulp lasted for three years under the editorship of Frederick Pohl and Alden H. Norton, returning for a further 15 issues between January 1949 and August 1951. It published the first stories by James Blish and Chad Oliver, as well as promoting the work of Isaac Asimov and L. Sprague De Camp. The bold and colorful covers were unsigned, but inside, Hannes Bok and Virgil Finlay contributed to the magazine's generally successful era.

By the 1950s, the surviving pulps were all being turned into digest-sized magazines, and what few new ones did emerge tended to hedge their bets with titles that emphasized fantasy rather than sci-fi. Avon Periodicals launched *10 Story Fantasy* in the spring of 1951 with very high hopes. The editor was Donald A. Wollheim, whose contacts among the leading authors enabled him to garner new stories from Fritz Leiber, L. Sprague de Camp, John Beynon (a.k.a. John Wyndham), and Arthur C. Clarke with 'Sentinel of Eternity,' which would years later become the inspiration for Stanley Kubrick's classic movie *2001: A Space Odyssey.* Perhaps Wollheim got carried away with the response from these masters of sci-fi, because the magazine actually included 13 stories instead of 10! The cover was a bit of a surprise, too, featuring a whip-wielding fiend menacing a girl in a fur-edged bikini, which was probably unlikely to appeal to the more sophisticated new generation of sci-fi readers. In any event, a second issue of *10 Story Fantasy* never appeared.

Two years later the company tried again with *Avon Science Fiction Reader*, also edited by Wollheim. There was no new material in this pulp, only reprints

ABOVE RIGHT

Fred Anderson was another of the talented artists who made Planet Stories *so eye-catching on the newsstands. This cover illustration was for 'Temptress of Planet Delight' by Betsy Curtis. (Summer, 1948)*

ABOVE

The brass brassiere lives on! This unsigned cover for Super Science Stories *illustrates 'The Brain Beast' by William F. Temple. (July, 1941)*

SPRING 1951   25¢

10 STORY FANTASY

TYRANT & SLAVE-GIRL ON PLANET VENUS
by **John Beynon**

Franklin Gregory • August Derleth • A. E. Van Vogt • F. Leiber • and others

ABOVE

No credit was given to the artist who produced this cover for the only issue of 10 Story Fantasy. *The story was by John Beynon, now better known as John Wyndham.*

of classic sci-fi by Ray Cummings, Clark Ashton Smith, and Edmond Hamilton, plus Sewell Peaslee Wright's archetypal yarn from an earlier era, 'Sacrifice to the Lust Queen of the Flame Rite.' Today it is the wonderfully garish but uncredited covers of all three of these Avon magazines that make them collectors' items.

One further title, *Fantastic Story Magazine*, deserves a mention – if for no other reason than the cover of its fall 1951 issue pictures an ice-covered world with the planet Saturn looming on the horizon and looks uncannily like the very first issue of *Amazing Stories*. The pulp was a last fling from Ned Pines's Popular Publications with Sam Merwin Jr. in the editorial chair. It drew heavily on the archives of *Thrilling Wonder Stories* – occasionally reprinting even earlier material from the Gernsback era – augmented with some new work by Chad Oliver, A. E. Van Vogt (the first serialization of 'Slan'), and Henry Kuttner's 'A Million Years To Conquer.' Merwin did his best to generate reader enthusiasm in his column, 'Cosmic Encores' and the artwork provided by Paul Orban, Alex Schomberg, and the evergreen Virgil Finlay was, as might be expected, excellent to the end.

Fantastic Story survived until the spring of 1955. With its passing, sci-fi pulp disappeared into a black hole. It went largely unnoticed and unmourned in spite of the important role it had played in developing the century's latest and now hugely popular literary genre.

Sci-fi pulp disappeared into a black hole, largely unnoticed and unmourned – in spite of the important role it had played...

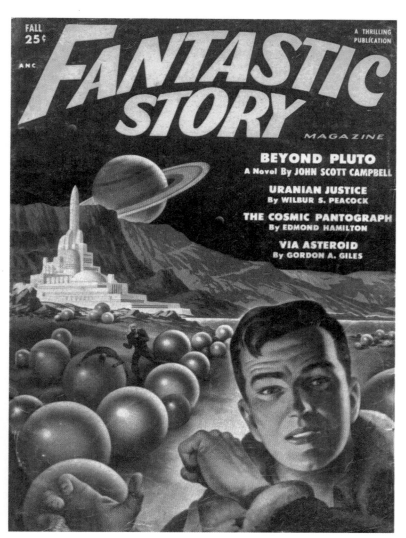

DARING DIANA

PAUL RÉNIN

The Chilling of Hotsy

THE BRIT PULPS

The publisher who introduced 'Yankee Magazines' into Britain was a former market stallholder from London's East End named Gerald G. Swan.

RIGHT

This girl was drawn by Reginald Heade for a cover of Hank Janson's, Hotsy – You'll Be Chilled. *(1951) (See page 196)*

OPPOSITE

Philip Simmonds was one of the earliest British pulp artists, and created cover illustrations for Paul Renin's notorious sex novels like Daring Diana. *(May, 1938)*

Swan was one of a group of quick-on-their-feet entrepreneurs – very much like those in the U.S. – who created what became known as the 'Mushroom Jungle.' They made their fortunes by flooding Britain with gaudy, provocative pulp magazines and paperbacks to entertain millions of readers in the postwar austerity of the 40s and early 50s. A lot of the action, adventure, and sex fiction that Gerald Swan and his fellow publishers peddled through the nation's smaller newsagents and bookstalls was sold (as in the States) U.T.C., and earned a notoriety that prompted police raids, court cases, and even imprisonment for some of those involved. Today, however, the British pulp magazine is a scarce item, and little is known of the lives of the men who made this piece of publishing history.

Philip Simmonds's pictures of teasing, sexy young girls would not have looked out of place on the covers of the pulps.

Gerald George Swan has been described as the 'Barnum of the British Comic Business,' and began his career in the 1920s, buying and selling kid's comics from a bookstall in the famous Church Street Market off the Edgware Road in London. All around him were a colorful array of stallholders: quack doctors, fortune tellers, and even the odd three-card-trick operator. Swan was a tall, bespectacled man who wore a grey suit and trilby hat at all times. He sold weekly comics at four a penny and monthly magazines, such as the detective series *Sexton Blake Library*, for a penny each, all of which were stamped with his trademark of a swan. When the magazine was brought back to the stall, half the cost was refunded. Comic book historian Bill Lofts, who grew up in Marylebone, London, remembered Swan well, 'He was a kindly man and always accepted my comics back however much they were tattered, and treated me with just as much courtesy as if I were a high paying customer.'

Lofts discovered that Swan, who came from a poor family, had borrowed 30 shillings from his mother to set up in business in 1921. The popularity of his exchange scheme grew rapidly, and he also began selling the American pulps being shipped across the Atlantic. (Later, a select few of the leading titles, such as *Argosy*, *Love Stories*, and *Black Mask*, would be reprinted under licence by distributors in the U.K.) These magazines were predominantly inoffensive adventure, western, crime, and romance titles, and Swan found they sold well to his customers. They also gave him an idea that would take a few years to realize.

Children's comics, however, continued as the biggest part of Swan's business, and after opening an office in nearby Edgware House, in Burne Street, his first ventures into publishing were three titles for the juvenile market, *New Funnies*, *Thrill Comics*, and *Slick Fun*. Swan also had the foresight to stockpile paper, so that when the Second World War broke out, and paper rationing came into force in February 1940, he had the raw material to feed the nation's craving for escapist entertainment during the uncertain times that followed. According to historian Steve Holland, who coined the term

'Mushroom Jungle' to describe the activities of Swan and his colleagues:

'This remarkable foresight meant that when war broke out, Swan had three warehouses stacked with magazines and books, which he gradually distributed throughout the early years of the War. Even the destruction of one warehouse – destroyed by fire in 1940 – was not enough to ruin him, and much of his success can be put down to the rush of titles he put on the market at the start of his career. Although best remembered amongst collectors for his many comics and juvenile papers, Swan's early output included several pulp magazines and 60 snappy novels by Paul Renin.'

With titles like 'London Night Haunts,' 'One Night in Paris,' 'Daring Diana,' 'All That Glitters,' and 'Sex' – all with covers by Philip Simmonds, a man whose pictures of teasing, sexy young girls in various stages of undress would not have looked out of place on the covers of the pulps – the Renin novels set Swan's embryo publishing empire on its feet. The French-sounding

RIGHT

Affinity, *the first of Gerald G. Swan's pulp magazines, was illustrated by an artist who signed himself (or herself) C. Holland. (May, 1946)*

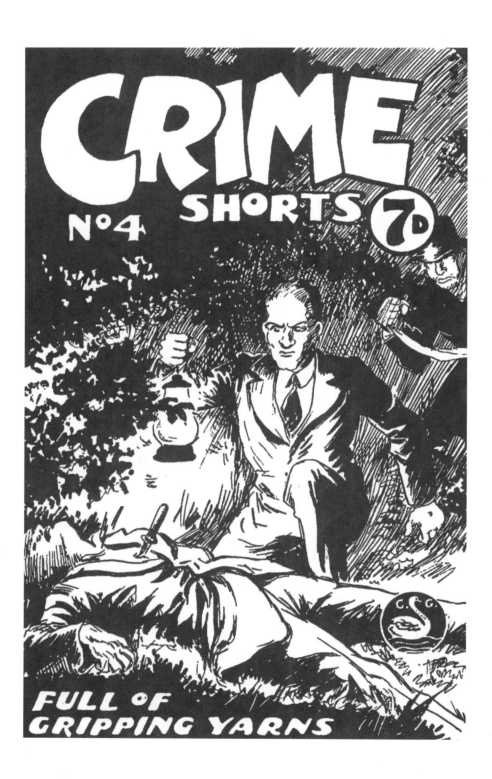

name of the author only added to the suggestiveness of their contents. The blurb for *Sex*, published in 1928, for example, was typical of its kind:

'Sex has never played the vital and open part in the life of the nation that it does today ... What of the young men and girls who are lured from the fireside by distant, seductive callings to learn romance and its moods for themselves in the little corners of the city where night steals early and danger lingers always? These are the human, poignant problems with which Paul Renin tells a daring story of romance, of passion, of lovers old and young, of great emotions and greater need.'

The author Paul Renin was, in fact, British – Richard Goyne, the son of a vicar. He had studied at the Royal College of Music before becoming a freelance journalist and producing millions of words for publishers like D. C. Thomson and their line of weekly romance magazines, including the hugely popular *Red Letter*. When Swan decided to launch his first pulp magazine, a romance title, *Affinity*, in 1939, Renin, a.k.a. Goyne, was an obvious contributor. He was in all probability the author behind 'No Ties For Trixie' by 'Kay Simnett,' 'Nightmare Face' by 'Gerald Evans,'

'What of the young men and girls who are lured from the fireside by distant, seductive callings to learn romance and its moods for themselves...?'

'A Man on her Mind' by 'Carlton Mills,' and other stories under names that appeared in the magazine. *Affinity*, with its colorful, romantic covers by C. Holland, had an immediate sales appeal in gloomy, wartime London. Holland's work was augmented inside the pulp by several other anonymous illustrators, whose work for the women's magazines had dried up when many titles became casualties of the wartime restrictions.

Unhappily, the high standard of artwork in *Affinity* was not repeated when, in 1941, Swan realized his dream of publishing his own versions of the American pulps that had sold so well on his stall. The titles chosen had a definite American feel to them and, to underline the fact, they were all referred to as 'Yankee Magazines' – a term Swan himself coined. In quick succession, he launched *Detective Shorts*, *Crime Shorts*, *Gang Shorts*, *Occult Shorts*, *Vengeance Shorts*, and *Yankee Shorts* – the last one of which mixed just about every kind of short story – crime, horror, adventure, and romance. He bought reprint rights for stories from several of the U.S. pulps, including *Black Mask* and *Weird Tales*, as well as recruiting a team of his own writers. Among them were Edwy Searles Brooks, who had written countless stories for Amalgamated Press, the prolific actor-turned-author William J. Elliott, a young man named Trevor Dudley Smith, who would ultimately become famous as the best-selling thriller writer 'Elleston Trevor,' and, most prolific of all, Norman Firth, who became known as 'The Prince of Pulp Peddlers.'

Firth was one of the most extraordinary figures in British pulp, a man whose output matched any of his contemporaries in the U.S. in terms of variety and the number of words he turned out. Born in Birkenhead in 1920, the son of a theatrical producer, Firth worked as an assembler in an aircraft factory before making his earliest sale in 1945 to Swan's *Crime Shorts* No. 4. The story was 'Professional Killer,' the first of a series about a hardboiled professional killer, Merrick Lawrence, with his own hedonistic view of life. The opening paragraph revealed that Firth had little to learn from his hardboiled compatriots across the Atlantic:

OPPOSITE
The crude style of E. H. Banger illustrated the vast majority of the Swan pulps, including Crime Shorts *No. 4, which published Norman Firth's first story, 'Professional Killer.' (1945)*

'So that's how I came to set up as the man to eliminate the yobs who wanted eliminating anyways...'

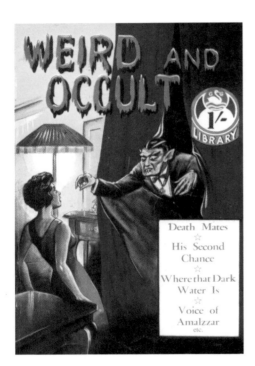

'Professional Killer, that's me, and I ain't over interested in the fact that you consider I'm a sort of cross between a snake in the grass and something which crawls outta rotten woodwork. I toted a gun for "Baby Face" Nelson back in the old days, and I'll allow there wasn't a strong-arm man who was any slicker on the draw than yours truly. Then the Feds got on to Nelson and took him away for a free holiday in the pen at the expense of Uncle Sam, so I packs my grip and takes it on the lam, pronto. It is at this moment in my career that I decides what a sucker I've been toting a gun for saps who were too yellow to do their own shooting, and getting nothing but pin-money out of it in the bargain. So that's how I came to set up as the man to eliminate the yobs who wanted eliminating anyways...'

Once published, Firth never looked back, and dashed off millions of words of detective stories, westerns, romances, science fiction, and snappy fiction for Swan, and many of the other London pulp publishers that followed. Tragically, in 1949, he contracted tuberculosis and died, aged just 29. It has been estimated by his biographer, Steve Holland, that Norman Firth produced in excess of five million words in just five years of writing.

When it came to choosing artists for his magazines, Swan earned himself a notoriety that he never lost. The most prolific of his artists was E. H. Banger, who had drawn cartoon strips before providing the crude, single-color covers for Swan's entire pulp line. Rarely were these magazines illustrated inside. The one exception was *Weird Story Magazine*, which featured the work of Michael Stimpson, another artist whose background in drawing juvenile comic strips was all too obvious in his work. The pulp lasted just one issue. Curiously, though, it is their very crudeness that has endeared the Swan magazines to modern collectors!

The threat of German bombs falling on London, combined with the scarcity of paper, meant that Swan had few

ABOVE LEFT

The Swan pulps burst into color – this is an unsigned front cover illustration for Weird and Occult Stories, *a series that began in 1946.*

competitors in the pulp market until the tide of war began to turn in 1944. One rival was Modern Fiction Ltd., based in Holloway in North London, an operation that had been set up to import American magazines, but instead of launching its own line like Swan, went into the paperback market with a series of short gangster novels, all clearly influenced by the pulps. One of its most popular writers was 'Griff,' a pen-name that hid the identity of Ernest McKeag, a juvenile publications editor at the Amalgamated Press, who moonlighted for several 'Mushroom Jungle' publishers. McKeag's mastery of the come-on title – *From Dance Hall to Opium Dive*, *I Spit On Your Grave*, and *Brooklyn Moll Shoots Bedmate* are typical examples – plus the curious period cover art of Ray Theobald, as stylized in its way as that of E. H. Banger, made the Modern Fiction paperbacks become very collectable today.

The same can also be said of Utopian Publications, which operated from Gloucester Mansions in Cambridge

ABOVE

Ray Theobald was a British pulp artist who moved easily through the different genres, and from paperbacks to magazines like this Modern Fiction *title, 'Brooklyn Moll Shoots Bedmate.' (March, 1951)*

STRANGE OFFSPRING

AMERICAN FICTION No. 10
RAYMOND A. PALMER
ONE SHILLING NET

STRANGE TALES

WEIRD AND FANTASTIC FICTION
FIRST SELECTION   ONE SHILLING NET

contacts, Gillings was able to buy the rights to stories from the U.S. pulps by American authors including Jack Williamson, Edmond Hamilton, and Robert Bloch, and these formed the contents of Utopian's first two homegrown pulps, *Strange Offspring* (sci-fi) and *Strange Fantasy* (Weird and Fantastic Fiction). Gillings later reflected on these magazines:

'With few exceptions, the shiny covers consisted of genuine art studies of full-breasted ladies in provocative poses. They were modest booklets, priced at one shilling, though only a few of the cover girls wore flimsy draperies that left precious little concealed.'

Circus, London. The company was founded by Benson Herbert, an ex-schoolteacher with a penchant for American pulp science fiction, who had previously worked for a London publisher, Lloyd Cole, producing lurid novels with titles like *Strange Romance* and *Bedtime*. Recruiting an old friend, Walter H. Gillings, who was also a sci-fi fan and had edited a short-lived English magazine, *Tales of Wonder*, before the War, Herbert sensed an opportunity to profit from the American experience. Utopian Publications would combine scientific imagination with good old-fashioned titillation. Through his

What enabled Benson and Gillings to get away with this unabashed nudism – although all traces of pubic hair were carefully airbrushed out – was the argument that they were being published to provide 'light relief' (take that how you will) for the troops – especially U.S. soldiers based in the U.K., many of whom were familiar with the authors. The War Office, it is said, turned a blind eye to this sly deception. Occasionally, *Strange Tales* used two-color artwork on the cover. These illustrations were all the handiwork of Alva Rogers, who showed a modest talent for voluptuous female figures.

ABOVE LEFT
Strange Offspring *was not a nudist magazine, but a pulp full of American science fiction stories! (January, 1946)*

ABOVE RIGHT
Strange Tales, *a companion pulp to* Strange Offspring, *carried covers illustrated by Alva Rogers.*

'With few exceptions, the shiny covers consisted of genuine art studies of full-breasted ladies in provocative poses.'

In 1945, Utopian Publications issued two more pulps, *Thrilling Stories* and *Strange Love Stories*, adhering to the same formula. However, with the emergence of several new pocket-size science fiction magazines – particularly *New Worlds* and its companion *Science Fantasy* from Nova Publications in Stoke Newington – the company dropped *Strange Offspring* and *Strange Fantasy*, and decided instead to concentrate on crime and western novels. A later brief return into the pulp market, in 1948, with *Paris Nite Life*, *Spicy Stories*, and *Harlem Hotspots* – almost single-handedly written by Norman Firth – were notable mainly for the unique covers by Reina M. Bull, one of the few female British pulp artists. Born in London, and with aspirations to become a fashion designer, Reina had begun her career providing dust-jacket illustrations for several small London book publishing houses before finding a steady stream of work with Benson Herbert. Subsequently, she moved on to her most successful period with *New Worlds* and *Science Fantasy*.

The uncertainty of the British pulp market caused the fortunes of Utopian Publications to fall as dramatically as they had risen, and Benson Herbert's only sure way of making money became selling prints of the photographs from *Strange Offspring*. By the end of the decade, Utopian was publishing only girlie magazines, with titles like *Fads and Fancies* and *Outdoor Antics* – all full of 'French models' and 'lingerie poses.' Benson can claim to have invented the 'Readers' Wives' page, now so popular in semi-porn magazines – although there was not a great deal of excitement to be had from the photographs he published of thin, often embarrassed females showing off their camiknickers. The end for this pulp pioneer was very different from that of Gerald G. Swan, who retired a wealthy man. According to Steve Holland, Herbert's premises were raided by the police and he would be fined as much as £200 a time. 'Even his competitors stole his photographs to sell them,' Holland has written, 'and finally it was a case of 'too many fines and too many thieves.'

Science·Fantasy
WINTER 1951-52   TWO SHILLINGS

RMB

Another pulp publisher who made his mark at this time was William C. Merrett. He was the owner of a printing business at 335 City Road, in London, which meant he had a regular allocation of paper. Very little is known about Merrett or the authors and artists who contributed to his two 'WCM Publications,' *Verity* and *Crime Detective.* No authors were listed in either magazine for the stories, with their evocative titles, such as 'Riddle of the Corpse in Lovers Lane,' 'Sex Maniac,' 'The Actress and the Killer,' and 'Underworld Terror.' And the unknown artist who painted the cover pictures of dishevelled young women either wielding whips or being subjected to bondage undoubtedly set a benchmark for the British pulps.

In 1945, with the Second World War rapidly drawing to a close, there was a sudden rise in the number of new publishers – all with their eyes fixed on the opportunities that peace would bring. Although paper rationing would not be lifted until June 1953, these enterprising men always managed to obtain supplies from somewhere. The odds on success were shortened considerably when a ban was placed on importing periodicals from the U.S. – pulps included – because of the balance of payments problem with the dollar.

Two London publishing families, the Assaels and the Babanis, who had been associated since 1942 in Bernards Publishing, a company producing technical manuals about electronics and radio, decided to branch out into the

ABOVE LEFT
The artwork on the excellent covers of Crime Detective *was, as on its companion pulp,* Verity, *unsigned.*

ABOVE RIGHT
No artist is credited for this cover of Verity *published by William C. Merrett in the mid 40s.*

OPPOSITE
Reina Bull was another of the select band of female pulp artists. She rose to fame illustrating the covers of Science Fantasy. *(*Winter, 1951*)*

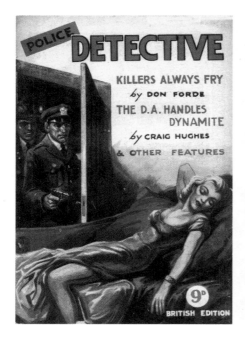

ABOVE

The expression of the girl on this Police Detective *cover makes it seem likely she is expecting visitors! No artist is credited. (June, 1949) (See page 193)*

ABOVE

Jack Brabbins was a talented English artist who brought the Wild West alive on the covers of Rip-roaring Western. *(August, 1948)*

popular marketplace. Albert Assael set up Bear Hudson Ltd. on Goldhawk Road, London, and Hamilton & Co (Stafford) Ltd. in a converted shop not far away in Melville Court. Both companies planned to publish fiction and non-fiction titles, their size and page length dependent on the amount of paper available at any time. Bernard Babani founded Brown Watson Ltd. at premises in The Grampians at Western Gate. His intention was more specific: to publish 32-page pulp magazines featuring the popular themes of western tales, detective stories, and spicy confessions. Within a year, Sol Assael, a relative of the Bear Hudson founder, joined forces with Michael Nahum to launch John Spencer & Co. and publish crime titles and sexy pulps. Later, this company would become notorious for their series of sci-fi and fantasy paperbacks issued under the Badger Books imprint.

Bear Hudson was the first to release any titles – several hardboiled crime novels by Coolidge McCann and Elmer Elliott, who were both the same person, Frank Dubrez Fawcett. Fawcett was another very prolific author of the era, now best remembered as the creator of the feisty blonde Miss Otis in the Ben Sarto paperback novels, *Miss Otis Comes to Piccadilly*, *Miss Otis Says Yes*, *Miss Otis Throws A Comeback*, and

> Bear Hudson's most **successful** pulp, *Rip-roaring Western*, carried a **phoney price** of 35 cents on the cover to try to **convince** customers of its **American** origin.

many more. As Coolidge McCann, he was one of the main contributors to Bear Hudson's most successful pulp, *Rip-roaring Western*, which carried a phoney price of 35 cents on the cover to try to convince customers of its American origin. The artwork – among the best on any British-published western – was by Jack Brabbins, a man who had actually never been nearer the old Wild West than the New Forest in England.

Hamilton & Co targeted three markets with its quartet of pulps, launched in 1946: *Police Detective*, *Crime Investigator*, *Strange Adventures*,

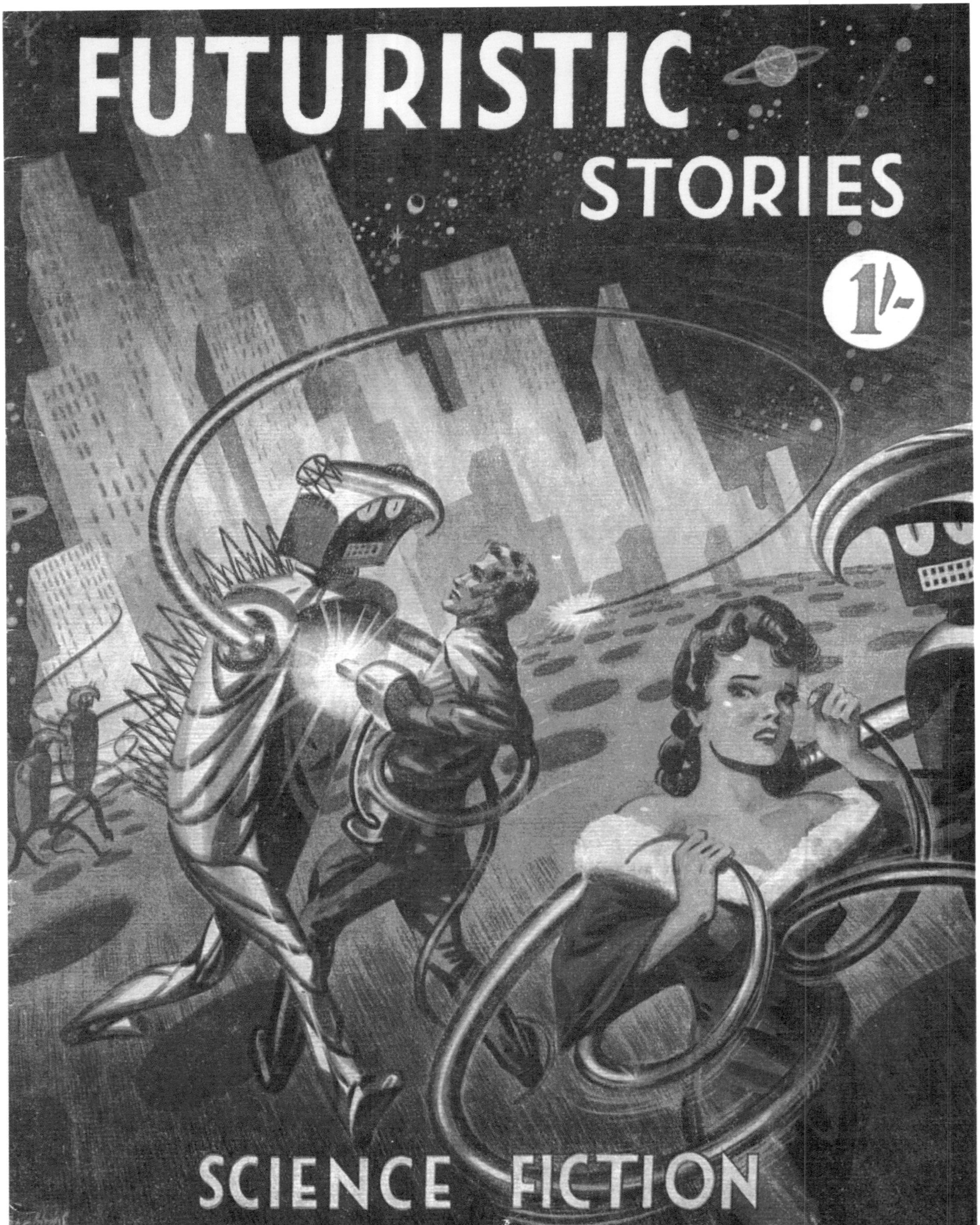
FUTURISTIC
STORIES
1/-
SCIENCE FICTION

and *Futuristic Stories*. Again the evidence suggests that Fawcett and Norman Firth were the main writers for these magazines. Most of the stories in *Police Detective*, such as 'Killers Always Fry' by Don Forde and 'The DA Handles Dynamite' by Craig Hughes, were set in the U.S., as were the short, factual articles, such as 'Dry Land, Adieu' (Prohibition) and 'To Sleep, Perchance To Dream' (Drugs). The cover art was by John Pollack. The fiction was of much the same kind in the companion pulp, *Crime Investigator*, although there was the occasional local tale of detection to be found, for example J. Ernest Roland's 'Your Dab, Sir?' and 'Lady on the Run' by David Andrews.

Despite its title, *Strange Adventures* actually offered a mixture of fantasy and science fiction. One tale, credited by name to Norman Firth, 'Mary Had A Little ...' provides a good indication of the writer's versatility because it is described in the blurb as 'a riotously funny story about the thing that followed Mary about, a thing from another dimension.' The companion pulp, *Futuristic Stories*, was sci-fi pure and simple, with the emphasis on simple. It ran a series by Rice Ackman about a character named the 'Space Hobo,' whose exploits included 'Space Hobo's Diary,' 'The Timeless Dimension,' and 'Dark Asteroid,' set on Neptune, a very curious planet full of metal men with quiffs.

Undistinguished as *Futuristic Stories* was, the interest it generated prompted Hamilton & Co. to publish *Authentic Science Fiction* five years later. The editor, Gordon Landsborough, became one of the first important postwar paperback editors. *Authentic* is regarded as something of a landmark in

'...a riotously funny story about the thing that followed Mary about, a thing from another dimension.'

OPPOSITE

British science fiction pulps, such as Futuristic Stories, *lagged far behind the sophistication of their American counterparts. (October, 1946)*

ABOVE RIGHT

This early example of the talent of Josh Kirby illustrates Brain W. Aldiss's story 'Out Of Reach,' for Authentic Science Fiction Monthly. *(August, 1957)*

Aida Reubens was a cinema pianist who had lost her job with the advent of talking pictures. After composing verses for greeting cards, she switched to writing fiction.

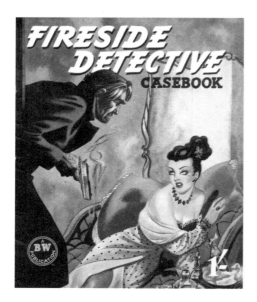

ABOVE
*Neither the
authors nor
illustrators who
contributed to*
Fireside Detective
Casebook *were
credited.
(February, 1948)*

U.K. science fiction, for having started to popularize the work of three important writers – Brian W. Aldiss, E. C. Tubb, and William F. Temple – as well as featuring artwork by John Davis (who was, for a time, the magazine's art editor) and Josh Kirby, today one of the best known artists in the fantasy field for his covers on Terry Pratchett's phenomenally successful *Discworld* novels.

Brown Watson's trio of crime pulps, *Fireside Detective*, *Bedside Detective*, and *Keyhole Detective* all appeared in 1946, but once again gave no credit to the authors of '15 Minute Alibi,' 'It's Been A Long Time,' and a rather Agatha Christie-like mystery, 'Crime Comes To Chimneys.' The hand of Norman Firth is suspected. The one exception was Kenneth David Westwood, author of the David Bartley detective stories that were published in *Keyhole Detective*. Other 'BW Publications' of the time included *Western Star Adventures*, *Sparkling Confessions*, *Superb Confessions*, and *Tantalizing Tales*. It has recently been established that quite a number of the short stories written for Brown Watson magazines were by Aida Reubens. She was a cinema pianist who had lost her job with the advent of talking pictures. After composing verses for greeting cards, she switched to writing fiction, and tackled just about every theme from thrillers to first-person 'confessions.'

John Spencer & Co. arrived on the pulp scene in the summer of 1946 with its *Crime Confessions* series. Here, yet again, the majority of the stories were by Norman Firth. But what undoubtedly put this magazine head and shoulders above the competition was the cover artwork by Reginald Heade, whose voluptuous and brazenly erotic girls were the equal of any to be seen in the U.S. Heade was to become famous for his association with the hardboiled novels of Hank Janson, but it was his initial work for pulps such as *Crime Confessions* that helped to create his legend as a master of pulp art.

Although the name of Reginald Cyrie Webb Heade is familiar to all those with an interest in 'Mushroom Jungle' publishing, little is known about the man himself, beyond the facts he was born in 1903 and died in Hammersmith in 1957, leaving no family and no will.

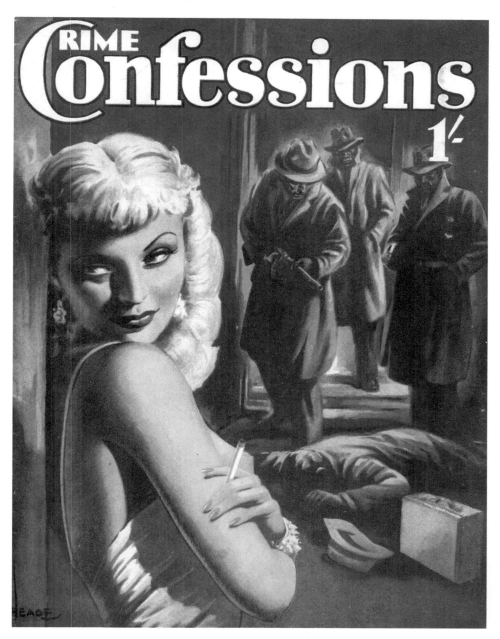

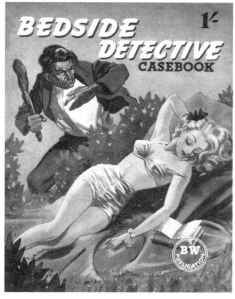

ABOVE

The cover art for this issue of Crime
Confessions *was provided by Reginald
Heade, Britain's greatest pulp artist.
(June, 1948)*

RIGHT

Bedside Detective Casebook *came from
the same publishing house as* Fireside
Detective Casebook, *and similarly failed
to acknowledge any of its contributors.
(March, 1948)*

RIGHT

This is one of Reginald Heade's classic covers for one of the famous Hank Janson series of paperback novels, Hotsy – You'll Be Chilled. *(1951)*

OPPOSITE

Philip Mendoza was the illustrator for the Hank Janson story, 'Double Double Cross' in Underworld Magazine. *(April, 1951)*

Francis had created a hardboiled newspaper reporter with an eye for hard cases and easy women.

He apparently became an illustrator in the late 30s, concentrating on books and annuals for children and doing occasional richly colored portraits of demure ladies and their adoring lovers for the covers of romantic novels. Heade's dramatic change from coy maidens to smoldering, cigarette-smoking beauties is believed to have occurred after he saw some U.S. pulps, and realized it was a style he could master. What is certain is that once Heade's 'good girl art' (as it became known) started appearing on covers, such as *Crime Confessions*, he was instantly in demand.

The landmark year in his career was 1948, when he was contacted by Stephen Francis, an author and publisher based at 267 Gray's Inn Road, London, who was planning a series of gangster novels. Francis had created a hardboiled newspaper reporter, with an eye for hard cases and easy women, named Hank Janson, and wanted someone to illustrate the jacket of the first title, 'This Woman in Death.' The oil painting Heade delivered, of an exotic blonde in a figure-hugging black dress cut to the waist, was sensational. The artist also designed the distinctive lettering for 'Hank Janson,' based on his own signature. The book became an immediate bestseller, established Janson's character, and led to Heade producing a further 59 covers for the legendary series.

Not surprisingly, these books, with their arousing covers, became enormously popular (if usually furtive) reading with a whole generation of schoolboys, of which I was one. However, the increasingly daring covers – with the appearance of girls whose clothes had been ripped almost to the point of nudity, like the beauty on *Hotsy – You'll Be Chilled* – brought the books to the attention of the authorities. It was not long before a number of booksellers and distributors were raided by the police, and in the autumn of 1953, several of them had their entire stocks of Hank Janson titles seized. Following a decision to prosecute Francis, the police also confiscated many thousands of Heades covers, which were ordered to be destroyed. As a result of the subsequent trial at the Old Bailey, several people involved in the Hank Janson publishing venture were given prison sentences. Reginald Heade escaped this attention, but Steve Chibnall, an authority on his work, has speculated that the artist himself may well have been visited by the police and given a warning: certainly he never again painted one of his exotic beauties. For the few remaining years of his career, Heade contented himself with producing artwork for paperback biographies and stories of high adventure, which he signed simply, 'Cy Webb.'

Another element of the Hank Janson legend, almost forgotten today, is the pulp magazine *Underworld*, which

'Right under my nose, almost touching my face, was a dainty, high-heeled shoe with a dainty foot inside it.'

Stephen Francis launched in 1951. Aimed at cashing in on the success of the paperback novels, it nevertheless only had a typographical cover with the unmistakable 'H. J.' initials printed large. *Underworld* ran short stories about Janson as well as reprints of stories by classic U.S. writers whom Francis admired, including Damon Runyon, O. Henry, and Jack London. A typical Janson saga, 'Double Double Cross,' opened in the style that was familiar to the millions of readers of the paperbacks, Hank having once again been beaten unconscious by a gangster:

'My eyes opened slowly and reluctantly like I'd been sleeping at least 20 years. Right under my nose, almost touching my face, was a dainty, high-heeled shoe with a dainty foot inside it. The ankle was delicately shaped and it wore a slender, golden chain. But there was something wrong about looking at a dame's foot. Because the only way you can see a dame's foot that close is when you're lying on the floor. And why should I be lying on the floor?

'I didn't feel very strong. I tried to move my arms and they were stuck. My feet were stuck, too. It seemed as if my muscles weren't working. Then I realized I was tied hand and foot. I could manage to move my head – a little – and again it was the slim legs I saw.

But much more clearly this time. Again my eyes traveled upwards, but my perception was heightened. Black lace step-ins, the creamy flesh showing through the openwork, strained tightly over slender hips and a broken thread of cotton where a tiny button had broken away, unable to take the tension. As she looked down at me she rested her hands on her hips. That posture tautened the muscles of her body, giving emphasis to the sharp out-thrust of her breasts. "Feeling stiff?" she asked …'

Although the cover was innocuous, *Underworld* had superb interior artwork by Philip Mendoza, a former newspaper illustrator, whose skill at drawing beautiful women from an amazing variety of angles made him ideally suited to the magazine. Apart from this work, Mendoza also produced cover artwork for a number of paperback publishers, notably the Danny Spade series for Scion Ltd., about a crime reporter who doubled as a private eye and was clearly an imitation of Hank Janson. Mendoza signed these pictures as 'Ferrari.' The stories themselves were written by Dail Ambler, an author who had worked for a number of romantic magazines before throwing off the shackles of that genre to tackle crime fiction, which she did with considerable success.

The Dame Plays Rough

Danny Spade

ONE SHILLING & SIX PENCE

Ferrari

Alongside *Crime Confessions*, John Spencer also published *Phantom Detective Cases*, with stories by Firth ('Killer at Coney'), Leslie Halward ('Some Joke'), and someone who called himself 'Superintendent Maryin.' He or she probably had nothing to do with the police, although the tale of 'The Scarred Killer' was more accurate on police procedure than most other crime fiction of the time. The artist Frank Taylor provided the best of the magazine's covers. A pulp called *Harem Frolics* was Spencer's stab at emulating the American spicy magazines, and he tried to strengthen the impression by printing a '75 cents' price tag on it. The publishers also attempted to heighten reader expectation with a claim on the cover that it contained 'Artist Models.' But this was actually the title of a story inside by Will Norman.

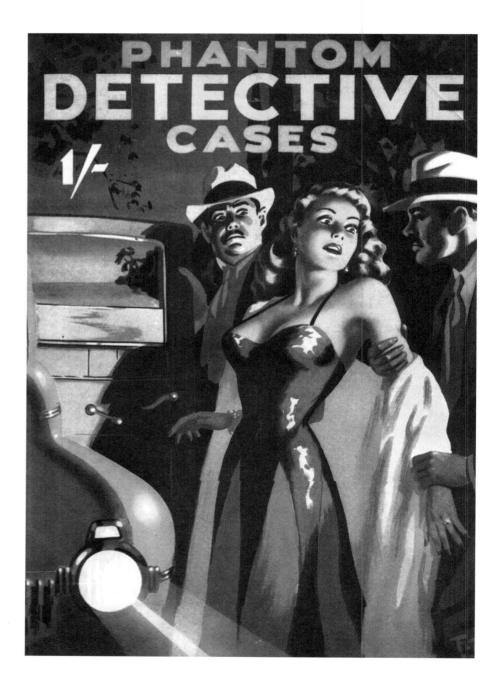

ABOVE LEFT
Printing American prices on the covers of British pulp magazines like Harem Frolics *was a common practice in the late 40s. (Summer, 1948)*

ABOVE
This striking Frank Taylor cover is in the best American pulp tradition for Phantom Detective Cases. *(February, 1947)*

The nearest rival to Reginald Heade among the other illustrators of British pulp magazines was certainly H. W. Perl, whose alluring girls in see-through dresses and negligées were a great sales draw for the publications of Grant Hughes. Based at 131 Brackenbury Road in London, the company had been launched in 1946 by D. A. Fletcher and Joseph Pacey. It utilized the talents of Norman Firth and three other wordsmiths, Dennis T. Hughes, Frank Griffin, and John Rafferty, to fill their pulps *Crime Stories* and *Gangster Pay-Off*. As with Reginald Heade, we know little about Perl beyond his name and the fact that, after his heyday in the 50s, he completely disappeared from the publishing scene. The delicacy of the skin tints and the diaphanous nature of the clothing worn by his girls became the trademark of his work, and it is now as keenly collected as that of Reginald

LEFT
H. W. Perl illustrated this cover of Crime Stories. *He was the only British artist to threaten seriously the supremacy of Reginald Heade as a pulp cover illustrator. (1948)*

The publishers also attempted to heighten reader expectation with a claim on the cover that it contained 'Artist Models.'

ABOVE LEFT
*Several French-style pulps, such as
Gaieté!, were priced in francs by their
English publishers, no doubt to raise
expectations! (September, 1948)*

ABOVE
*The cover of this novel is
illustrated with another of
H. W. Perl's unmistakable
lovelies. (1948)*

...both Perl and Heade always put any male characters well to the rear of their beautiful girls, seemingly so as not to disturb their equilibrium.

Heade. Interestingly, both Perl and Heade always put any male characters well to the rear of their beautiful girls, seemingly so as not to disturb their equilibrium and in marked contrast to the American conformational style.

The trick of putting phoney foreign prices on the covers of pulps was also used by several other English pulp publishers, notably Scion Ltd., The Park Trading Company, and Paget Publications. Scion, based at 37a Kensington High Street, was founded in 1947 by Binyimin Immanuel, a Latvian who had come to Britain to escape the menace of Hitler. His first publication was a pin-up booklet about Rita Hayworth and the success of this – it sold more than 200,000 copies – encouraged Immanuel to branch out into comics, crime novels, spicy magazines, and ultimately science fiction. One of Scion's first titles was *Gaieté*! which was priced on the cover at 100 francs, but actually cost 2s 6d. Neither the cover artist nor the writers of the fiction inside were credited.

Scion made perhaps its biggest mark in publishing with science fiction, issuing a series of paperback novels by Vargo Statten who was, in fact, the British writer John Russell Fearn, who had been contributing to the U.S. pulps since before the War. Titles such as *Operation Venus* (1950), *The Micro-Men* (1950), and *Deadline to Pluto* (1950) thrust Statten, Scion, and the man who illustrated the covers, Ronald Turner, into the public eye. Ultimately, the series of 52 Vargo Statten titles sold in excess of 5 million copies. Turner had learned his craft working for Odhams Press and began his association with Scion by drawing for the comics. But he found his real niche when he was commissioned to paint the Vargo Statten covers. He took great care with these pictures and admitted to being influenced by the famous American space artist, Chester Bonestall. Turner's finest work was arguably for the *Vargo Statten Science Fiction Magazine*, which Scion launched in January 1954 edited by Alistair Paterson. It carried fiction by John Russell Fearn writing as Vargo Statten, as well as short stories under another of his pen-names, Volsted Gridban.

The mixture of fiction and factual articles enabled the *Vargo Statten Science Fiction Magazine* to flourish for a year, but then Paterson's insistence that authors should keep their stories

'If you can take your eyes off that cute little number on the cover, take my tip and try the stories.'

simple for an unsophisticated audience made it impossible to attract the top names in the field. Even a title change to the *British Space Fiction Magazine* and a reduction in size to digest format could do nothing to halt its eventual demise. Today, copies with Ron Turner's covers are more sought after than the fiction inside.

The Park Trading Company unashamedly hijacked Gerald Swan's catch phrase to promote its line of pulps as 'Yankee and French Magazines.' The firm was based in Portland Road, in London (but claimed – unspecified – addresses in New York and Paris), and priced its French look-alike pulps, *Latin Night Life*, *Forgotten Virtues*, and *Girls of Desire* at '100 francs' and the American-orientated companions *Whisper*, *Flirt*, *Eyeful*, and *Beauty Parade* at '25 cents.' All in fact sold at

two shillings. The writers for all of the Park Trading magazines were probably pseudonyms: Gerald Kent ('Posed in the Nude'), Ben Horton ('He "Maid" Her'), and Nat Kerby ('The Caliph's Daughter'). The general editor was Tony Lee, who adopted a cheerful, matey tone in an editorial in *Latin Night Life*:

'Hi Fellers! This is it. The magazine you've been waiting for. If you can take your eyes off that cute little number on the cover, take my tip and try the stories. You like the idea? I thought you would. What are you waiting for?'

Lee also wrote some of the short stories that appeared in the magazine and showed he had little to learn from his American counterparts. Take this extract from 'Nights of Passion':

'Her arms had been upon his waist and as he pulled his body away from hers, she let her hands drag round until they pressed his stomach. The feeling of them made him tense, hold himself still, waiting. Her hands moved lower and his passion reared, red hot and violent.

'Savagely he pulled her body against his, his arms under hers and his hands reaching up to the warm whiteness of bare shoulders. Their lips met and she returned his burning kiss with perhaps even greater fervour. Their thighs pressed together, Tex felt her stomach moving in and out against his, felt those glorious breasts boring into his chest, felt a knee forcing itself between his legs.'

Latin Night Life was also something of an oddity in the pulp market in that it ran 'foldout' color pictures of semi-

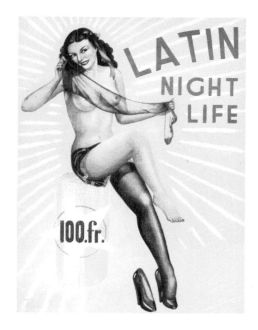

naked girls by the cover artist who signed himself 'Parker.' It also promoted a 'Lonely Hearts Club' – promising 'Confidential, Dignified, Honest Service' with its own 'Hostess' Betty Webb.

Paget Publications in Netheravon Road, London, was another busy imprint that initially entered the marketplace in the postwar years with comics for children, such as *Paget's Tupney* and *Paget's Dandy Tupney*. In the late 40s and early 50s they produced a number of pulps including *Paget's Western* (1948), which was shortly afterward joined by rather more spicy material in the 'Candid Series.' Some of the titles were little more than euphemisms for the female anatomy – *Jewel*, *Daub*, and *Kitty* – while others were frankly bizarre: *Rippling*, *Plink*, *Spick*, *Winsome*, and even *Droop*! A group of anonymous hacks filled the

ABOVE

An illustrator who signed himself 'Parker' drew the covers of Latin Night Life, *which was 'priced' in francs. (1948)*

ABOVE

Ron Turner was the most accomplished British artist in the sci-fi field, and provided a series of exceptional covers for the Vargo Statten Science Fiction Magazine, *including this, the first issue. (March, 1954)*

pages of these magazines, a feature of which were the inside cover phonographs of rather wholesome, topless models. Just as Benson Herbert had done before, Paget Publications offered 'Fine Art Studies' for 'Art Students or Admirers of the Female Form,' which came in a sample dozen priced at £1.

The Gannet Press in Birkenhead, near Liverpool, was one of the few pulp publishers to operate outside London. For several years it prospered with a line of western, crime, romance, and science fiction paperbacks, before making a brief foray into the pulp market in 1955 with a fantasy magazine, *Weird World*. The publication was a mixture of the classics – Edgar Allan Poe's 'The Fall of the House of Usher' appeared in the second issue – along with some bizarre thrillers by contemporary writers: 'Woman Running' by Justin Croome, 'There Are Harps in Hell, Too' by Charles E. Price, and 'The Charlady Who Traveled Faster Than Light' by Anthony Righton. *Weird World* ran the occasional poem and even tried to promote new talent with a 'Grand Short Story Competition.' What made this pulp memorable, however, was the fantasy artwork of Roger Davis, who drew all the covers and most of the interior illustrations in a style not that far removed from Virgil Finlay. His beautiful women were similarly tastefully concealed by shadows, flowers, or wisps of cloth.

Two more British companies, Curtis Warren and Muir-Watson, flirted briefly with pulp magazines in the early 50s,

before the paperback boom replaced them just as it had done in the U.S. Curtis Warren, which operated from Holbex House, in Lambs Conduit Street, London, is best remembered for its sci-fi novels, although their early publications were crime and detective pulps. Run by Edwin Self, who also acted as editor, Curtis Warren apparently had an association with Hamiltons and Grant Hughes, as a number of the authors and artists who provided material for all three were able to disclose. Manuscripts sold to one were quite likely to appear under the imprint of another, while artwork commissioned by Grant Hughes would occasionally be reused on Curtis Warren books! In a classic case, a piece of Frank Taylor artwork depicting a bound and gagged beauty being menaced by two gangsters appeared on the Curtis Warren cowboy pulp *Western Crime Stories*. Authors who wrote for this magazine included Lee Dexter, Morton T. Cayne, and Bevis Winter. *Detective Crime Stories* was a short-lived companion publication to which the same writers also contributed.

Muir-Watson was even further away from the heart of the 'Mushroom Jungle' at 112 Bath Street, in Glasgow. The company was founded in 1948 by two partners, John Muir and John Watson, the latter an R.A.F. flight lieutenant who won a D.F.C. during the War. Trained as a journalist on *The Glasgow Herald*, John briefly tried to run an arts magazine before deciding that romance and crime pulps might be a better bet. The first titles were *My Confession* and *True Love*, for which John himself wrote

Roger Davis's beautiful women were similarly tastefully concealed by shadows, flowers, or wisps of cloth.

'...a fierce story of an unforgettable woman whose passion men couldn't forget...'

tales such as 'Small Town Girl With Big Ideas,' 'Flying Into Cairo,' and 'Dime for a Dance.' Both magazines had covers featuring up-and-coming film stars, such as Joan Bennett and Ann Miller. However, what put Muir-Watson on the map – and ultimately led John Watson to leave Glasgow to become managing director of the Mayflower paperback line in London (and, incidentally, one of my closest friends in publishing when I was editorial director at New English Library) – was his creation of the hardboiled writer, Nat Karta. John told me years later:

'Someone in the trade said I was wasting my time pissing around with romances. What the public wanted were gangster novels with the hint of a lot of f---- going on, like those by Ben Sarto and Hank Janson. So I sat down and wrote one called The Merry Virgin and called myself Nat Karta. One of the biggest distributors, Thorpe & Porter, promptly agreed to buy 50,000 Nat Kartas a month. So I went right ahead and invented a couple more writers, Hans Vogel and Hyman Zore. After that, I was in the money.'

John Watson was a master of the selling blurb. He put a photograph of himself on the inside front cover and declared without a hint of false modesty:

'Nat Karta is one of the few writers who has this highly developed gift of making readers share every breathtaking thrill, every pulsating incident, each voluptuous moment in his unorthodox adventures. Only his authentic background – for years he was one of America's trouble shooting crime aces – has made possible the stark, virile underworld dramas that have put him in the top ranks of *Tough Gangster Writers*.' [John's italics.]

In describing some of the best-selling titles in the Nat Karta series he wrote:

'*The Tigress Bites* – "a fierce story of an unforgettable woman whose passion men couldn't forget"; *Bravely To Bed* – "Karta writing about the snatch racket gives fiction a new authenticity"; and

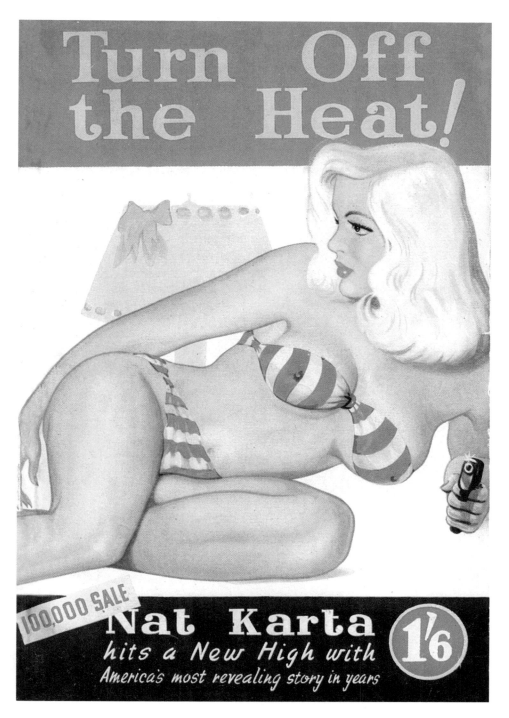

Eat Me If You Must – well, what needs to be said about that!'

The goodtime girls and gangsters' molls who appeared on the Muir-Watson covers were the work of an exuberant Glasgow artist, David Waite, who favored large bosoms and smoldering, over-the-shoulder glances. When John Watson himself was unable to keep up with the demand for the Karta, Zore, and Vogel novels, he employed a rota of freelance authors including Norman Lazenby, Vic Hansen, and Richard Hutton.

John commented a few years ago shortly before his untimely death:

'They were publishing-on-the-run days. We only used writers who could turn in thousands of words a day, and so if some of the stories read like crap then they probably were crap. There was no time for rewriting. The same went for the pulp magazines. They all had to have flashy covers and sexy girls to sell. As far as all the publishers were concerned, anything went as long as it made money and didn't bring the law knocking on the door.'

John Watson's words are perhaps a fitting epitaph for all of those who lived and worked during the Classic Era of the Pulps on both sides of the Atlantic.

OPPOSITE
Film stars like Joan Bennett were used on the covers of the Muir-Watson pulp My Confession, *which was full of risqué love stories.*

ABOVE
This voluptuous cover by David Waite was for one of the last stories in the Nat Karta series, and aptly titled Turn Off The Heat. *(1949)*

PARIS NIGHTS
THE MERRY WHIRL OF THE WORLD IN STORY AND PICTURE

25¢ MAY

When Two Reform

By Therese F. Dupree

RARE ART POSES PAR EXCELLENCE

The Pulp Wordsmiths

APPENDIX

The writers who produced the uncountable millions of words for the pulps were an amazingly diverse group of men and women.

RIGHT

This cutout image is taken from Tom Greiner's cover for Paris Gayety. *(March, 1934)*

RIGHT

This cutout image is taken from Tom Greiner's cover for Paris Gayety. *(March, 1934)*

OPPOSITE

Reading was not high on the list of the desires of the girls in the sexy pulps – which makes this cover by Tom Greiner for Paris Nights *something of a rarity! (May, 1933)*

Some pulp authors were unabashed hacks trying to make a quick buck, and their work has deservedly gone into oblivion. Other authors became household names. In the pages of the pulps, genuinely talented writers learned the craft of storytelling, and it is no surprise that many of their serial stories have been reprinted in book form, while their short tales have frequently been anthologized in collections of crime, horror, and science fiction. For the interest of younger readers, who may not be familiar with their names, here are details of the most significant of the 'pulp wordsmiths.'

ASIMOV, ISAAC (1920–1992)

Born in Russia, Asimov emigrated to the US with his family, and discovered the science fiction genre – of which he would become one of the 20th century's prime exponents in the pulp titles on sale in his father's candy store in New York. His first short story, 'Marooned off Vesta,' appeared in *Amazing Stories* in 1939. Asimov's fame was assured with the long-running and highly influential series of *Robot* and *Foundation* novels.

BALLARD, W(ILLIS) T(ODHUNTER) (1903–?)

A prolific writer for the crime and Western pulps under numerous pseudonyms, W. T. Ballard's most famous character was the hardboiled private eye Bill Lennox, for *Black Mask*. He later wrote a series of popular crime novels with Hollywood and Las Vegas settings.

BELLEM, ROBERT LESLIE (1894–1968)

Described as 'The Shakespeare of the Spicys,' Bellem was a former Los Angeles newspaper reporter, radio announcer, and film extra. He became one of the most productive writers of pulp sex fiction and was equally skilled at creating love stories as those of lust and perversion, occasionally using pen-names – of which Justin Case is one of the few to have been identified. The character that made Bellem famous was Dan Turner, a tough, wisecracking Hollywood private eye. He made his debut in *Spicy Detective* in 1934 and later had his own magazine, *Hollywood Detective*. After the demise of the pulps, Bellem wrote scripts for T.V. shows like *Dick Tracy*, *77 Sunset Strip*, and *Superman*. Recently there has been talk of a major movie about Turner.

BLASSINGAME, WYATT (1909–?)

Born in Alabama, Blassingame worked on newspapers before breaking into the pulps with the help of his brother, Lurton, an author's agent. Wyatt wrote more than 400 stories for 50 publications and later became a writer of reference works and children's books as well as a teacher of creative writing.

BLOCH, ROBERT (1917–1994)

Famous as the author of *Psycho* (1959), which was brilliantly filmed by Alfred Hitchcock, Bloch became an enthusiast of horror fiction after reading *Weird Tales*, and was particularly influenced by the work of H. P. Lovecraft (q.v.). Apart from his contributions to *Weird Tales*, he was a also a regular contributor to *Strange Stories*, where he used a pen-name, Tarleton Fiske. He subsequently published numerous collections of stories that had first appeared in the pulps and was the winner of several awards, including a Hugo in 1958.

BRADBURY, RAY (1920–)

Born in Illinois, Bradbury, who is now regarded as one of the supreme fantasy writers of his generation, was an avid reader of the pulps and was first published in the pages of *Weird Tales*, where he made a total of 25 appearances. These stories were later collected, and several formed the basis of the novels that established his reputation, including *The Martian Chronicles* (1950), *The Illustrated Man* (1951), and *Fahrenheit 451* (1966) – all of which have been made into movies.

BRAND, MAX (1892–1945)

This was the pen-name of Washington-born Frederick Schiller Faust, who wrote more than 30 million words for the pulps under a variety of aliases, and has been described as 'The King of the Pulps.' His fiction ranged from Westerns to weird stories, and his prolific career was tragically brought to an end when he was killed in Italy while he was serving as a war correspondent.

BROWN, FREDRIC (1906–1972)

Although he is best remembered for his mystery novels, Fredric Brown began his writing career contributing to the detective pulps, and followed this with sales of stories to *Weird Tales* and *Unknown*, where his black humor and clever use of puns made him very popular with readers. One of the collections of his short fiction tales, *Nightmares and Geezensticks* (1961), is considered to be a classic.

BURKS, ARTHUR J(OSH) (1898–1974)
A former lieutenant in the army, Burks gave up his career when he discovered his ability to write quickly for any market, which made him a natural pulp author. He was named the 'Speed Merchant of the Pulps,' although he only occasionally felt the need to employ pen-names, such as Estil Critchie and Spencer Whitney. Very little of his work has been collected, and the full extent of his output will probably never be known.

BURROUGHS, EDGAR RICE (1871–1950)
The Chicago-born creator of the immortal Tarzan and the space hero John Carter of Mars, Burroughs was another prolific writer who made his debut in *All-Story Magazine*, using the pen-name Norman Bean. He later contributed to various other pulps, including *Amazing Science Fiction*, and his fame has never diminished thanks to the continued reprinting of his books about the ape man of the jungle – who has also, of course, featured in dozens of movies and television series.

CAVE, HUGH B(ARNETT) (1910–)
Born in Chester, England, Cave emigrated with his family to the US when he was five years old and he began contributing to pulp magazines while he was still at college. His ability to switch genres made him popular with editors at *Weird Tales*, *Strange Tales*, and *Dime Mystery*. He later lived in Haiti, where he studied voodoo, before moving to Jamaica, where he established a coffee plantation and wrote the occasional horror story.

CAIN, JAMES M(ALLAHAN) (1892–1977)
A former lecturer and newspaperman in his native Maryland, Cain began writing for the pulp fiction magazines in his spare time, and then became famous overnight with the publication of his crime novel, *The Postman Always Rings Twice* (1934). He was awarded a Grand Master Edgar by the Crime Writers of America in 1969.

CAMPBELL, JOHN W(OOD) JR. (1910–1971)
A fan of the sci-fi pulps from their inception, Campbell sold his first story 'When The Atoms Failed' to *Amazing Stories* in 1930. Under the pen-name Don A. Stuart, he wrote the short story 'Who Goes There?' in 1938, which has twice been filmed as *The Thing From Outer Space*. In 1937, he became editor of *Astounding Stories*. From then until his death, he played a vital role in developing the talents of some of the finest US sci-fi writers.

CHANDLER, RAYMOND (1888–1959)
Born in Chicago, but educated in England, Chandler was a successful executive in the oil industry until the years of the Depression. To earn some money, he began to write for pulp magazines, in particular *Black Mask*, for which he produced 20 novelettes. Several of these later formed the basis of his famous novels about the hardboiled private eye Philip Marlowe. The publication of *The Big Sleep* (1939) ensured his lasting fame, as well as his continuing influence on the crime genre.

CLARKE, ARTHUR C(HARLES) (1917–)
A giant of modern sci-fi, Clarke was born in Somerset, England, and was active in fan circles before making his first sale to *Astounding Science Fiction* in 1946, with 'Rescue Party.' He wrote stories under the pen-name Charles Willis before focusing on novels and building his reputation. This effectively began in 1951, with *Prelude to Space*, and was enchanced with the adaptation of his story 'The Sentinel' into the classic movie, *2001: A Space Odyssey* (1968) directed by Stanley Kubrick.

COBLENTZ, STANTON A(RTHUR) (1896–1982)
A poet and book reviewer, Coblentz made his debut as a sci-fi writer with 'The Sunken World' in *Amazing Science Fiction* in 1928. For the next decade he contributed a variety of similar stories of life in alien environments, which made him one of the most popular sci-fi writers of the time.

OPPOSITE
*Erle Stanley
Gardner sold some
of his first work
to* Breezy Stories, *which also
numbered Dorothy
Quick and Paul
Ernst among
its regular
contributors. The
excellent cover
artist of this issue
was given no
acknowledgment.
(June, 1936)*

COOPER, KEN(NETH) (1906–?)

This New York-born writer and former newspaperman took advantage of the pulp magazines' insatiable demand for fiction, and wrote prolifically for the various spicy titles and others of the same kind. Cooper was adept at quickly providing stories of sex and sadism, which helped to make his name something of a by-word in the genre. He is believed to have continued writing, under other names, for several periodicals and paperback companies after the closure of the pulps.

CORYELL, JOHN RUSSELL (1848–1924)

As a staff writer for Street & Smith Publications in New York, John Russell Coryell was given the basic concept for Nick Carter, the boy detective, and launched the sleuth's long-running career in September 1886. The stories always appeared under the pseudonym 'By the author of Nick Carter,' and dozens of other writers have carried on what Coryell began in magazines, serials, and paperbacks.

COXE, GEORGE HARMON (1901–?)

After leaving school in New York, Coxe worked in a lumber camp and car factory before becoming a writer. He sold his first fiction to *Detective Story Magazine*, and subsequently wrote tales of sport, love, adventure, and the sea for dozens of the other pulp magazines. Later, he became a screenwriter in Hollywood, as well as writing a series of hardcover mysteries featuring Kent Murdock, a Boston newspaper photographer.

CUMMINGS, RAY(MOND) (1887–1957)

Made famous by the success of his novel *The Girl in the Golden Atom*, which was serialized in *All-Story Magazine* in 1919, Cummings became a popular contributor to Hugo Gernsback's pulp *Amazing Stories* after its launch in 1926. It has been estimated that Ray Cummings contributed more than 750 stories, under various pen-names, to pulp magazines in various genres.

DALY, CARROLL JOHN (1889–1958)

Credited with writing the first 'hardboiled story,' 'The False Burton Combs,' for *Black Mask* magazine in 1927, Daly's reputation was ensured shortly afterward when he began the series of stories and novel-length tales about the tough and ruthless crime-buster Race Williams. Despite the enormous popularity of Williams for almost a decade, Daly was later unable to sell any of his fiction, and moved from his native New York to California, where he wrote comic books.

DAVIS, FREDERICK C(HARLES) (1906–)

Described as 'one of the pulp speed demons,' Davis was estimated to have written in excess of a million words every year during the peak of the pulp era for the leading crime and mystery magazines. He started writing while still at Dartmouth College, in England, and became one of the highest-earning writers in the field. As well as his short stories, Davis wrote the adventures of a number of series characters, including Secret Agent X and Operator #5. After the pulps closed down, Davis wrote several mystery novels for *The Crime Club*.

DENT, LESTER (1904–1979)

From 1933 onward, this New York-born author wrote almost 200 adventures of the great pulp magazine hero Doc Savage, under the pen-name of Kenneth Robeson. Later, he tried to write a series of crime novels using his own name, starting with *The Red Spider* (1968), but these enjoyed nothing like the success of his square-jawed superhero.

DERLETH, AUGUST W(ILLIAM) (1909–1971)

Born in Wisconsin, Derleth wrote his first horror story, 'Bat's Belfry,' when he was only 13 – although it was not published until he was 17, in *Weird Tales*. He rapidly became one of the leading lights in the horror genre and, as well as publishing and promoting the work of H. P. Lovecraft (q.v.) after his death, via his publishing

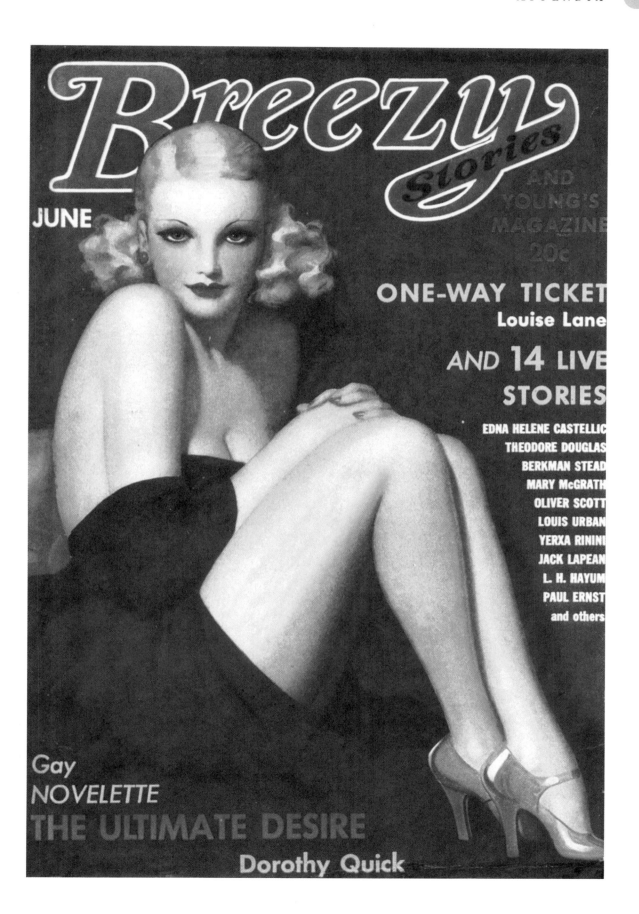

imprint, Arkham House, Derleth also wrote prolifically for a number of the pulps. Many of his stories were later assembled in collections, such as *Not Long For This World* (1948) and *Dwellers in Darkness* (1976).

ERNST, PAUL (1900–)

Having spent much of his youth traveling, Ernst was well equipped with the raw material for fiction, and with the advent of the pulps he was soon one of the elite band of writers, producing about a million words per year. He particularly enjoyed writing horror stories – making his debut in *Weird Tales* in 1928 with 'The Temple of Serpents.' He also wrote a series for the magazine about an evil genius known only as 'Dr. Satan.' Ernst later wrote 23 issues of *The Avenger* pulp, and contributed to a number of the slick magazines, before retiring to live in Florida.

FARLEY, RALPH MILNE (1887–1963)

Farley, a Harvard-educated teacher, engineer, and later state senator, wrote under the pseudonym of Roger Sherman Hoar. In the 20s, he began contributing to a number of the pulps, including *Argosy* magazine, for which he wrote 'The Radio Man' (1924), featuring the exploits of the intrepid Miles Cabot. Such was the success of this character that Farley continued his adventures in a series, which ran until the 50s.

FEARN, JOHN RUSSELL (1908–1960)

This English writer began his career contributing to the American pulp *Amazing Stories* – his first sale being a superman-type story, 'The Intelligence Gigantic' in 1933. He also wrote for *Astounding Science Fiction* and several pulps in other genres, using his own name and various pseudonyms. Following the acclaim he received for a series about a female superwoman 'Violet Ray, The Golden Amazon,' which began in *Fantastic Adventures* in 1939, Fearn gathered a whole new readership in Britain. He went on to produce a string of novels under the pen-names of Vargo Statten and Volstead Gridban.

FISCHER, BRUNO (1905–)

A New York journalist and former editor of the *Socialist Call* magazine, Fisher was one of the most adept writers of weird menace stories, and contributed more than 50 stories, primarily to the *Popular Publications* titles, most of which were published under the name of Russell Gray. Fisher was famous in the business for being the writer who could be shown an existing piece of cover artwork and produce a short story to match the following day.

FISHER, STEVE (1912–)

Born in California, Fisher spent four years in the US navy, where he wrote more than 200 articles for navy publications before moving to New York in the 1930s. Here, his flare for writing action-packed crime stories enabled him to sell to pulps like *Black Mask.* Later he moved to Hollywood, where he became a successful screenwriter for films and television, receiving five Emmy Award nominations. Fisher also wrote several mystery novels, as Stephen Gould, and in 1967 contributed to the book *The Pulp Jungle*, by his friend and fellow-writer, Frank Gruber (q.v.).

GALLUN, RAYMOND Z(INKE) (1911–)

Aged only 19 when he published his first story, 'The Space Dwellers,' in *Science Wonder Stories* (1929), Wisconsin-born Galiun later went on to contribute to *Astounding Science Fiction*, where he introduced his 'Old Faithful' series about a friendly Martian. He adopted a number of pen-names during his most productive period, between 1929 and 1942, and following the demise of the pulps has written a few novels, including *The Planet Strappers* (1961) and *The Eden Cycle* (1974).

GARDNER, ERIE STANLEY (1889–1970)

Described as 'one of the best-selling authors of all time,' Gardner was born in Massachusetts and, after training for the law, won a considerable reputation as a defender of the underdog. Writing always attracted him, however, and in 1923 he began contributing to the pulps – selling some of his first tales to *Breezy Stories* and *Snappy*

Stories. He quickly displayed his versatility, writing fiction for *Argosy*, *Black Mask*, and *Cowboy Stories*, among many others. His fortunes changed forever when he wrote a novel, *The Case of the Velvet Claws* (1933). In this, he introduced the now famous criminal attorney Perry Mason, who was to become the subject of dozens of further books, as well as films and a long-running television series.

GOODIS, DAVID (1917–1967)

Born in Philadelphia, David Goodis took a degree in journalism, and then wrote advertising copy for a local agency before moving to New York in 1939. There, he wrote horror stories, mysteries, and Westerns for Popular Publications under a variety of pen-names, and at one time was said to be writing as much as 10,000 words per day. His first novel, *Dark Passage* (1946), was filmed starring Humphrey Bogart, and led to a screenwriting contract with Warner Brothers. However, this proved an unhappy experience for Goodis, who returned to fiction. His later novels are now enjoying fresh acclaim.

GRUBER, FRANK (1904–1969)

It was in the Midwest of America, where he was born, that Gruber learned how to write, while working on a number of trade journals. He found his niche with the development of the pulps and wrote in most genres, from mystery to the Wild West. Gruber used many pen-names, and created several memorable characters, including Oliver Quade, 'The Human Encyclopedia,' and the tough private eyes Johnny Fletcher and Simon Lash. Gruber later wrote scripts for movies and television, and produced an insider's view of *The Pulp Jungle* (1967).

HAMILTON, EDMOND (1904–1977)

Credited with being one of the most influential figures in the development of sci-fi in America, Hamilton's first publication, 'The Monster-God of Mamurth,' appeared in *Weird Tales* in 1926. His space opera stories became very popular in several of the science fiction pulps, where he used a series of pen-names, including Robert Castle,

Hugh Davidson, and Robert Wentworth. Hamilton also wrote as Brett Sterling for the popular Captain Future stories, which appeared in their own pulp magazine from 1940 to 1944. His later work, for *Startling Stories*, has been collected in book form, and he wrote a number of sci-fi novels, of which *A Yank at Valhalla* (1973) is regarded as the best.

HAMMETT, DASHIELL (1894–1961)

Former Pinkerton's agent turned writer and novelist, Hammett was writing advertising copy for a jewelry store when he began contributing fiction to *Smart Set* and its companion pulp, *Black Mask*. By 1927, he had become one of the most popular contributors to the crime magazine, with his hardboiled detective stories. It was these, when revised, that became his first novels, *Red Harvest* and *The Dain Curse* (both published in 1929). The novels that Hammett wrote in the next decade established him as the greatest of all the hardboiled crime writers, and his popularity has grown with each passing year.

HARRIS, JOHN BEYNON (1903–1969)

Better known as 'John Wyndham,' Harris was born in England but was first published in the US by *Wonder Stories*, which carried his 'Worlds to Barter' in 1931. He contributed to several of the sci-fi pulps under the names of John Beynon, Lucas Parkes, and Johnson Harris, before settling on the pen-name John Wyndham after the Second World War. He then wrote a string of popular novels, including two enduring classics, *The Day of the Triffids* (1951) and *The Kraken Wakes* (1953).

HEINLEIN, ROBERT A(NSON) (1907–1988)

Acclaimed as one of the pre-eminent figures in sci-fi, from 1940 to the 1960s, Heinlein was a naval officer, but he was forced to leave the service because of ill-health. He then proceeded to help generate a golden era for his chosen genre, contributing first to *Astounding Science Fiction*. He then wrote a series of stories, all part of his awesome 'Future History' concept. Heinlein's fame was assured with *Stranger in a Strange Land* (1961), which won a Hugo award, as did *The Moon is a Harsh Mistress* (1966). These and subsequent works earned him the accolade of 'Best All-Time Author' in many polls.

HOWARD, ROBERT E(RVIN) (1906–1936)

This Texas-born author, famous for his creation of Conan the Conqueror, was a puny child who took to body-building to enhance his physique, and then devoted his literary energies to writing about brawny superheroes. His first published story was 'Spear and Fang,' which appeared in *Weird Tales* in 1925, and he contributed many more yarns to the pulps about boxing, adventure, the West, and other genres. He was a prolific writer, but his career was brought to a sudden end when he committed suicide after the death of his mother. August Derleth (q.v.) was the first of several publishers who helped to bring Howard's work back into print and confirm his reputation.

HUBBARD, L(AFAYETTE) RON(ALD) (1911–1986)

Famous today as the founder of scientology, Hubbard wrote fiction for a number of the pulp magazines, coming to readers' particular attention with his science fiction and fantasy stories in the pages of *Unknown* and *Astounding Science Fiction*, where he displayed great skill as a storyteller. 'Typewriter in the Sky,' which first appeared in *Unknown* in 1940, is widely considered to be one of his best works. Hubbard also wrote other fiction, under the pen-names of Frederick Engelhardt, Rene Lafayette, and Kurt von Rachen.

KANTOR, MACKINLAY (1904–)

Born in Webster City, Iowa, Kantor had a burning desire to be a writer from his teens, and made some of his earliest sales to the crime and mystery pulps while still a young man. In 1950, he wrote *Signal Thirty-Two*, which has been described as 'one of the best police procedural novels ever written.' However, it was his epic novel of the American Civil War, *Andersonville* (1955), that established him as an outstanding writer of mainstream fiction, and also won him a Pulitzer Prize.

KELLER, DAVID H(ENRY) (1880–1966)

It was while working as a psychiatrist in a mental hospital that Keller began contributing tales of fantasy and horror to the pulps. His debut story, 'The Thing in the Cellar,' for *Weird Tales* in 1932, revealed his insight into the unconscious mind, and this theme resurfaced in numerous subsequent tales for the same magazine and for *Strange Tales*. Legend has it that Keller was once challenged by Harry Bates, the editor of *Strange Tales*, to write a 'truly horrific story.' The author came up with 'The Dead Woman,' but the magazine folded before it could be published. When Keller then offered the story to *Weird Tales*, it was rejected as too shocking!

KUTTNER, HENRY (1915–1958)

Born in Los Angeles, Kuttner was a highly versatile author of fantasy fiction who wrote one of the most horrifying stories ever published, 'The Graveyard Rats,' which marked his debut in *Weird Tales* in 1936. His early work was clearly influenced by H. P. Lovecraft (q.v.), but later, in the pages of *Unknown*, it took on a more fanciful and entertaining style. Kuttner wrote under a variety of pen-names for the pulps, including Keith Hammond, Peter Horn, and Lewis Padgett. He died tragically young at the age of 42.

LEINSTER, MURRAY (1896–1975)

William Fitzgerald Jenkins, writing as Leinster Murray, proved to be influential in the development of sci-fi following the publication in 1919 of his first story, 'The Runaway Skyscraper' in *Argosy*. Several of his early contributions to the sci-fi pulps were under the name of Will F. Jenkins, but it was as Leinster that he scored his biggest success with 'The Forgotten Planet' in 1920. He is remembered today, in science fiction circles, by the epithet 'The Dean of Science Fiction.'

LOVECRAFT, H(OWARD) P(HILLIPS) (1890–1937)

Probably the most acclaimed and discussed horror writer of the 20th century, Lovecraft was a strange, reclusive figure who lived much of his life in Rhode Island, and was dead before his work was widely appreciated. His early stories appeared in amateur magazines, but following the acceptance of 'Dagon' by *Weird Tales* in October 1923, most of his subsequent fiction appeared in this horror pulp. Lovecraft revised a great deal of fiction by other writers at the expense of his own work. Only one book bearing his name appeared during his lifetime, *The Shadow Over Innsmouth* (1916) – but the subsequent founding of Arkham House by August Derleth (q.v.) resulted in the rescue of his fiction from the pages of the crumbling pulp magazines.

MACDONALD, JOHN D(ANN) (1916–1987)

Born in Pennsylvania, MacDonald began to write while serving with the US army in the Second World War. His first sale was of 'Interlude in India' to *Story Magazine* in 1943, while he was still overseas. It was followed, when he returned to America, by a host of adventure, fantasy, sport, science fiction, and mystery stories. Much of this work appeared under 'house' names, including Peter Reed, John Wade Farrell, Henry Rieser, and Robert Henry, which has made tracing his full output impossible. After the success of his first novel, *The Brass Cupcake* (1950), which sold more than a million and a half copies, MacDonald concentrated on thrillers, creating the popular private detective, Travis McGee.

MERRITT, A(BRAHAM) (1884–1943)

Though often referred to as one of the 'Patron Saints of Science Fiction,' Merritt's work was, in the main, fantasy, and began in 1917 with a little story entitled 'Through The Looking Glass' in *Argosy*. Although he initially studied to become a lawyer, insufficient funds forced Merritt to seek work as a journalist. He quickly rose to become the editor of the *American Weekly*, and

retained the position until his death. Merritt was fascinated by ancient legends, and had successes with stories like 'The Conquest of the Moon Pool' in 1919 and 'The Ship of Ishtar' in 1924. These were reprinted in *Famous Fantastic Mysteries*, resulting in him becoming the only author to have a pulp magazine devoted to his work, *A. Merritt's Fantasy Magazine*. All his novels and short stories have been reprinted, and two unfinished novels were completed by the artist Hannes Bok.

PAGE, NORVELL W(ALTER) (1904–1961)

Legendary in pulp circles for wearing a black cape and large black hat, like the fictional superhero The Spider, whose adventures he wrote, Page had worked as a publicity officer and newspaperman before becoming a leading pulp wordsmith. A very versatile writer, he also wrote for a number of the crime and mystery pulps. But his best work was undoubtedly reserved for *Unknown*, where he published several epic fantasies, including 'Sons of the Bear God' in 1939, a story of the legendary Prester John, and 'But Without Horns' in 1940. Remembered as something of an eccentric by his colleagues, he left the pulp field in the 40s, mysteriously declaring that he was going to work for the US Government in Washington.

PRICE, E(DGAR) HOFFMANN (1898–?)

A former soldier with the US cavalry who saw action during the First World War, Price brought firsthand experience to his fiction, and specialized in adventure fiction for the pulps during the 30s and 40s. His earliest sale was 'Rajah's Gift' to *Weird Tales* in 1925 – the first of 38 stories he wrote for the magazine. Price later wrote a number of excellent Oriental fantasies and, although he never visited China, was made an honorary citizen of San Francisco's Chinatown for his accurate and sympathetic portraits of Chinese people. In 1934, he collaborated on a story with H. P. Lovecraft (q.v.), 'Through the Gates of the Silver Key', and several collections of his pulp fiction have been issued, including *Far Lands, Other Days* (1975).

QUICK, DOROTHY (1900–1962)

Born in New York, Dorothy Quick worked first as a store assistant and then as an office clerk before turning her undoubted ability as a writer to good use by writing love stories, romances, and poetry for the pulps. She was also fascinated by the supernatural, and in the 30s and 40s wrote many stories for *Weird Tales* and *Unknown*, including a trilogy about a girl who experiences earlier lives, which was launched in 1939 with 'Blue and Silver Brocade.' Subsequently, she wrote a number of thrillers, the last of which, *Enchantment*, was published the year before her death.

QUINN, SEABURY (1889–1969)

Washington-born Quinn had the curious distinction of being the most popular writer in *Weird Tales* and an editor for the trade magazine for undertakers, *Casket and Sunnyside* at the same time. Trained in both law and medicine, Seabury Quinn was also a natural storyteller, and found a number of outlets for his fiction among the pulp magazines. But it was to *Weird Tales* that he contributed almost 150 stories between 1923 and 1952, a great many of them featuring his fussy little French occult investigator character, Jules de Grandin. Despite the other famous authors that contributed to the magazine, Quinn consistently topped the popularity polls with his stories of de Grandin's battles with supernatural foes, always aided by his faithful assistant, Dr. Trowbridge. In the 70s, the majority of these stories were collected together in a series of paperback anthologies.

REEVE, ARTHUR B(ENJAMIN) (1880–1936)

Although he first trained as a lawyer, New York-born Reeve turned to journalism, and during the course of his work became fascinated by the reports he heard of science being used in the detection of crime. This gave him the idea for a series about the scientific detective Craig Kennedy, whom he introduced in *Cosmopolitan* magazine in 1910. Reeve's first book about Kennedy, *The Poisoned Pen*, appeared the following year, and this was shortly afterward adapted for the screen as a silent movie serial. Reeve continued to write short stories and novels about Craig Kennedy until his death. One of his most acclaimed stories was *The Clutching Hand* (1934).

ROUSSEAU, VICTOR (1879–1960)

Born in London, Victor Rousseau was educated in South Africa, but got his first job in New York just when the golden era of the pulp magazines was beginning. He contributed to many of these popular publications, including *Ghost Stories*, *Weird Tales*, and *Strange Stories* – in the main using his real name, but occasionally appearing as H. M. Egbert. Rousseau subsequently produced a number of popular novels, notably *The House of the Living Dead* (1927) about an ingenious occultist, Dr. Martinus.

SALE, RICHARD (1911–1993)

A prolific writer for the pulps, Richard Sale was born in New York, but educated in Washington. Immediately after leaving university in 1933, he returned to New York and quickly found work in the magazine field, selling stories to many of the pulps as well as some of the top slicks, such as the *Saturday Evening Post*. In all, Sale penned more than 350 stories before joining Paramount Studios as a screenwriter in 1944. In later life, he worked as a director and producer on several movies, and wrote a number of best-selling novels, including *The Oscar* (1963) and *For The President's Eyes Only* (1971).

SMITH, CLARK ASHTON (1893–1961)

Born in California, Smith's name is forever linked in the annals of *Weird Tales* with that of H. P. Lovecraft (q.v.) and Robert E. Howard (q.v.) as a result of the popularity and variety of his work. His original ambition was to be a poet, and some of his early verse was published in *Weird Tales*. Then an admirer suggested that he should try writing fiction as well. His debut story, 'The Last Incantation' (1930), heralded a rare talent, and his subsequent 110 stories for the pulp were later assembled into a series of collections that have ensured his reputation as a master of weird fiction has continued. Like Lovecraft, with whom he corresponded, Smith lived much of his life alone. In spite of the acclaim he received as an author, and the popularity of his work, he virtually gave up writing in the late 30s, when his parents died, leaving him a wealthy man.

SMITH, E(DWARD) E(LMER) (1890–1965)

Described as 'The Father of Space Opera' because of his influence on the development of sci-fi in the US, Smith trained as a chemist and was nicknamed 'Doc' by his admirers due to the initials 'PhD,' which were added to his by-line when his stories began appearing in *Amazing Stories* in 1928. He possessed a wonderfully vivid imagination, and his first serial, 'The Skylark of Space,' was an instant success with readers, who enjoyed what would become a saga of the battles between hero-inventor Richard Seaton, and the villainous Marc 'Blackie' Du Quesne. When he had exhausted all the possibilities of this confrontation, Smith penned a new series about two intergalactic races, one good and the other evil, also at each other's throats, called the Lensman stories, which was first published in *Amazing Stories*, from 1934. The constant republication of both series has ensured the Doc's fame.

WILLIAMSON, JACK (1908–)

Born and raised in isolated homes in Arizona and New Mexico, Williamson's writing career was inspired by reading *Amazing Stories* and the tales of A. Merritt (q.v.). It is not surprising then that his first story, 'The Metal Man,' was published in *Amazing Stories*, in 1928, and was clearly an admiring imitation of Merritt's exotic style. Further contributions to this pulp, and *Science Wonder Stories*, enabled Williamson to develop his own storytelling voice. In 1934, he created the powerful 'Legion of Space' series for *Astounding Science Fiction*. This space opera tale of a group of four buccaneering astronauts helped to seal his fame. Years later, after returning to college and taking a BA, an MA, and a PhD with a study of H. G. Wells's early work, Williamson became a teacher. Since then, he has done a great deal to turn science fiction into a subject worthy of academic study.

WOOLRICH, CORNELL (1903–1968)

Born in New York, Cornell Woolrich spent the early years of his life traveling with his father, who was a mining engineer. He then settled in his native city with his domineering mother. Thereafter, Woolrich became a virtual recluse, escaping from his lifestyle only in his writing – which some critics have suggested is profoundly reminiscent of Edgar Allan Poe in its unrelenting grimness. His style was ideally suited to the pulps, and from 1934 onward he contributed crime and mystery stories to several of the leading titles. He published a number of these stories under the pen-name of William Irish, and it is generally agreed that his best work was written before 1957, when his mother died. Then the combined effects of diabetes and alcohol left him a ruined man. Woolrich's novels, *Phantom Lady* (1942), *Rendezvous in Black* (1948), and *Savage Bride* (1950) are rightly regarded as classics, and, since his death, many of his stories have been adapted for the screen and television.

ZAGAT, ARTHUR LEO (1895–1949)

Another extremely prolific writer, Zagat is credited with having written more than 500 stories for the pulp magazines. Formerly a commercial salesman, he discovered that it was easier to sell words to publishers than persuade people to buy other products. He made his debut as a pulp author in *Wonder Stories* in 1930 with his story 'The Tower of Evil,' and in 1939 wrote a post-holocaust series for *Argosy*. Entitled 'Tomorrow,' the series was set in America and is highly regarded in sci-fi circles. Zagat also wrote a number of the Operator #5 stories, and contributed to several of the crime and mystery magazines. Zagat's death in 1949 coincided with the demise of the golden era of the pulps, to which he had so ably contributed.

INDEX